UNIFORM STANDARDS OF PROFESSIONAL APPRAISAL PRACTICE

Applying the Standards

9th Edition

Dennis S. Tosh
William B. Rayburn

Dearborn™
Real Estate Education

This publication is designed to provide accurate and authoritative information in regard to the subject matter covered. It is sold with the understanding that the publisher is not engaged in rendering legal, accounting or other professional service. If legal advice or other expert assistance is required, the services of a competent professional person should be sought.

Publisher: Evan Butterfield
Development Editor: Amanda Rahn
Production Manager: Bryan Samolinski
Art Manager: Lucy Jenkins

Table of Contents

Standard 2—Real Property Appraisal, Reporting   35

Standard 3—Real Property and Personal Property Appraisal Review, Development And Reporting   49

Standards 4-10   57

Statements   61

Preface

Recognition and adoption of the Uniform Standards of Professional Appraisal Practice (USPAP) have resulted in significant changes in the appraisal profession. The uniform standards have established a minimum foundation on which both the development of an appraisal and a reporting of the results must be based. The USPAP has been adopted by all of the major appraisal organizations in the United States, and members of these organizations who desire to be designated and recertified by their organizations must show successful completion of a uniform standards course. State appraisal boards have incorporated the uniform standards into their statutes and, thus, violations of the standards have resulted in suspensions and revocations of appraisal licenses and certifications. Prelicensing education includes a minimum number of hours covering the USPAP; in addition, licensees must show the USPAP coverage as a prerequisite to license renewal. The financial regulatory agencies that oversee federally-related real estate transactions require compliance with the USPAP as the minimum standards on which other procedural and reporting requirements by an appraiser are based. Public agencies at all levels—local, state, and federal—have adopted the USPAP and added supplemental standards that must be followed by anyone employed by or working on behalf of such agencies.

In recent years significant changes have occurred in regard to both the types of appraisal assignments and the types of appraisal reports recognized by the USPAP. In addition, the standards rules are now much more specific as to what must be included in the various types of appraisal reports. In recent years, several new statements and a number of advisory opinions have also been added to the USPAP.

All real property appraisers must understand and be able to incorporate into their appraisal practice the suggestions and requirements contained within the USPAP. Anything less most certainly will result in a reaction by clients, and the intended user(s) of the appraisal report who are directly impacted by the results of the appraiser's activities.

While the uniform standards cover types of appraisal activities and reporting other than real property, the direction of this book is toward understanding the portion of the standards that explains the development and reporting of real property appraisals. In addition, review appraisal, as it relates to real property, also is discussed.

The text begins with a brief explanation of the background of the USPAP. How the Financial Institutions Reform, Recovery and Enforcement Act (FIRREA) of 1989 addressed the uniform standards as well as how state appraisal boards have included the standards in their statutes. The differences between the standards, standards rules, statements on standards, and advisory opinions are discussed.

The Preamble through Standard 3 of the uniform standards have the most direct impact on real property appraisers. Thus, these portions of the USPAP are fully explained in this text. Examples and illustrations are included to assist the appraiser in understanding how his or her appraisal practice is impacted by the uniform standards. Each of these chapters in the text is followed by review questions. On completing the appropriate readings, the review questions should be answered. Both answers to the review questions as well as explanations appear in Appendix B.

In addition to the uniform standards and standards rules, the Appraisal Standards Board (ASB) also publishes Statements on Standards. As of 2002, ten statements have been published and three of these have been retired. These statements are explained in the text to help the appraiser better understand how these statements impact his or her practice.

The text also contains 30 case studies. Case studies provide the reader with the means by which he or she can take what has been learned from studying the uniform standards and applying that understanding to appraisal problems and situations confronted by appraisers. Suggested answers to the case studies appear in Appendix C.

You will find Appendices D and E to be invaluable resources. Appendix D is a handy list of web addresses for eight appraisal-related organizations, while Appendix E offers contact information for all of the country's state appraisal boards. Both appendices are useful for research purposes, or if you are interested in joining an appraisal society or seeking licensing or certification in other jurisdictions.

On completing your study of this material, you should have a better understanding of the USPAP. Because the uniform standards are a living document and thus subject to change and update, you should keep abreast of the changes. A quick overview of the standards is not sufficient. The standards should be studied, notes should be made, and questions should be asked. If we hope to be looked upon as professionals, then we must understand and comply with our uniform standards.

The Uniform Standards of Professional Appraisal Practice are copywritten and promulgated by The Appraisal Foundation. They are subject to ongoing critique and to additions and corrections. The portions of USPAP appearing in this book are reprinted with the permission of The Appraisal Foundation.

Dennis S. Tosh, Ph.D., is a member of the finance faculty at the University of Mississippi where he holds the J. Ed Turner Chair of Real Estate and teaches in the areas of real estate finance and appraisal/valuation. He serves as a member of the teaching faculties for several state and national appraisal and financial organizations. Dr. Tosh is co-author of *Questions and Answers To Help You Pass The Real Estate Appraisal Exams,* as well as numerous other texts and materials covering various appraisal topics.

William B. Rayburn, Ph.D., MAI, CFA, is a member of the finance faculty at the University of Mississippi where he teaches courses dealing with real estate investment analysis, income property appraisal and corporate finance. He holds a doctorate in finance and has authored numerous articles on real estate and financial valuation. Dr. Rayburn is active in The Appraisal Institute, having served during 1993 as chair of the Body of Knowledge Committee and 1994 as chair of the Research Advisory Board.

Dr. Rayburn and Dr. Tosh are co-founders of FNC, Inc., a real estate information infrastructure company specializing in speeding loan decisions by converting paper to data for financial institutions. They also served as consulting editors on *Fundamentals of Real Estate Appraisal.*

Background

The Uniform Standards of Professional Appraisal Practice (USPAP) are based on an original set of standards developed in 1986–1987 by the Ad Hoc Committee on Uniform Standards. This committee was comprised of representatives of the eight major appraisal organizations in the United States. Each of these appraisal organizations has adopted the uniform standards and, as such, these standards have become recognized throughout the United States as the generally accepted standards of appraisal practice. In addition, the standards have been adopted by other appraisal organizations as well as by local, state, and federal agencies.

The standards are considered to be a living document. They can be altered, amended, interpreted, supplemented, or repealed by the Appraisal Standards Board (ASB) of the Appraisal Foundation after exposure to the appraisal profession, users of appraisal services and the public in accordance with established rules of procedure.

A current edition of the uniform standards (Preamble through Standard 3) is reproduced and explained in this text. As part of an effective appraisal practice, every appraiser should retain a current copy of the USPAP. The easiest and most dependable method of staying current with the uniform standards is by participating in the subscription service offered by the Appraisal Foundation. The subscription service will provide you with all information disseminated through the ASB. This information will include changes in standards, standards rules, statements on standards and advisory opinions. The current charge is $150 annually. Information in regard to the subscription service can be obtained from:

Appraisal Standards Board
The Appraisal Foundation
Suite 900
1029 Vermont Avenue, N.W.
Washington, DC 20005-3517
Phone: (202) 347-7722
Fax: (202) 347-7727
www.appraisalfoundation.org

The Financial Institutions Reform, Recovery and Enforcement Act

At the time the Financial Institutions Reform, Recovery and Enforcement Act (FIRREA) was signed into law (August 9, 1989), the USPAP had become recognized and accepted as the uniform standards of the appraisal profession. Included in Section 1110 of Title XI of FIRREA is the following statement:

> that real estate appraisals be performed in accordance with generally accepted appraisals standards as evidenced by the appraisal standards promulgated by the Appraisal Standards Board of the Appraisal Foundation;

All of the federal financial institutions' regulatory agencies have incorporated the minimum standards set forth in the statute (Title XI) in their final rules, while listing additional criteria that shall apply to all appraisals performed as required for federally related transactions. Of the appraisal reporting requirements cited in the final rules of the regulatory agencies, "conform to generally accepted appraisal standard as evidenced by the USPAP unless principles of safe and sound banking require compliance with stricter standards" is the first requirement mentioned. In addition to the federal financial institutions' regulatory agencies, other federal agencies as well as state and local users of appraisal services have used the USPAP requirement as the minimum for generally accepted appraisal standards.

State Licensing/Certification

Today, every jurisdiction has, by statute, a licensing/certification program in operation. The USPAP has been incorporated in the statutes that created the state licensing and certification of appraisers. In some jurisdictions, the USPAP has been incorporated in its entirety (Introduction through Standard 3 or Standard 5) in the appraisal law, while in other states the uniform standards are simply referenced by name. Thus, a violation of the various provisions contained in the uniform standards may result in disciplinary action by the state appraisal board/commission against an appraiser. Disciplinary action may result in either suspension or revocation of a license or certification. State regulatory authorities, therefore, expect appraisers to understand the uniform standards and abide by them. In addition, proof that an applicant has had an educational course covering the uniform standards is a prerequisite for licensing and/or certification in every jurisdiction. Jurisdictions also require an update on the USPAP as part of the continuing education requirement for license/certification renewal.

Table of Contents

The USPAP is comprised of the following sections:

Preamble
Ethics Rule
Competency Rule
Departure Rule
Jurisdictional Exception Rule

Supplemental Standards Rule
Definitions

Standards And Standards Rules
        Standard 1 - Real Property Appraisal, Development
        Standard 2 - Real Property Appraisal, Reporting
        Standard 3 - Real Property and Personal Property Appraisal Review,Development
             and Reporting
        Standard 4 - Real Property Appraisal Consulting, Development
        Standard 5 - Real Property Appraisal Consulting, Reporting
        Standard 6 - Mass Appraisal, Development and Reporting
        Standard 7 - Personal Property Appraisal, Development
        Standard 8 - Personal Property Appraisal, Reporting
        Standard 9 - Business Appraisal, Development
        Standard 10- Business Appraisal, Reporting

Statements On Appraisal Standards

Advisory Opinions

Glossary

Index

A sound real property appraisal practice should include the documentation and review procedure required in the applicable sections. Specifically, you should fully understand the Preamble and Rules; Standards 1 and 2 covering Real Property Appraisal, Development and Real Property Appraisal, Reporting; and Standard 3, Real Property and Personal Property Appraisal Review, Development and Reporting. In addition, Standards 4 and 5 (consulting) need to be understood if consulting work is part of your business practice (Standards 4 through 10 are covered on some state licensing examinations).

Standards

As you familiarize yourself with the uniform standards, you will note that the ten standards are very broad statements. In fact, they consist of only two or three lines of text. You also will recognize the relationship that exists between the various standards. Specifically, Standards 1 and 2 deal with the development of a real estate appraisal and the reporting of the appraisal. Standards 4 and 5 cover the same substantive aspects of real estate consulting and reporting. Standards 7 and 8 deal with personal property, while Standards 9 and 10 cover business valuation. Two of the ten standards are singular in terms of subject matter. Standard 3, Real Property and Personal Property Appraisal Review, Development and Reporting, and Standard 6, Mass Appraisal, Development and Reporting do not have a separate reporting standard as do the other four areas of coverage.

Standards Rules

All ten standards are followed by standards rules. These standards rules are much lengthier than the standards themselves and are intended to be very specific concerning what should be done to adhere to each standard. The organization of requirements set forth in the standards rules complements the appraisal process. Many of the standards rules are followed by explanatory comments, which further describe the intent of the standards rules and have the full force and effect of the standards themselves. While the standard could be thought of as a "skeleton" in terms of a broad statement, the standards rules serve the function of "hanging muscle" on the skeleton and give completeness to the standard.

Statements on Standards

In addition to the standards and standards rules, the ASB also publishes statements on standards. The purpose of these statements is to clarify, interpret, explain, and/or elaborate on the standards and the standards rules. Statements on standards also serve to assist appraisers, clients, users, and the general public in understanding the standards. The statements have the same weight as the standards rules and can only be adopted by the ASB after exposure draft and proper time for comments. Additional statements on standards will be forthcoming through the ASB. As of January 1, 1992, the ASB issues an annual update of the USPAP that includes the new statements adopted by the ASB during the previous 12 months. The Appraisal Foundation subscription service includes a copy of the annual update.

Advisory Opinions

Advisory opinions also are issued by the ASB. These opinions are considered by the ASB as informal responses to requests it receives for information. These opinions, while unenforceable, do not establish new standards; however, appraisers and users of appraisals should look to them as examples of how "peers in the profession" might view the correct application of the Standards. If you wish to receive an advisory opinion concerning a specific question or problem, direct your request to the Appraisal Standards Board, in care of the Appraisal Foundation at the address given previously.

Glossary

The Appraisal Standards Board has recently issued a Glossary as a form of "other communications." While not an integral part of the USPAP, as the Definitions section is, these words and phrases are considered common to appraising. The purpose of providing such a glossary is to show the similarities and differences between these words and phrases.

Preamble and Rules

The Preamble and Rules Section of the uniform standards sets the general tone for the responsibilities of an appraiser. In addition to the appraiser's responsibilities to his or her client, obligations also extend to intended users of the appraisal report as well. Specific issues covered in this portion of the USPAP should be fully understood by appraisers before they try to address and understand the specific topics covered in the ten standards. To do otherwise is perhaps "putting the cart before the horse."

The following subsections are included in this portion of the USPAP:

> Preamble
> Ethics Rule
> Competency Rule
> Departure Rule
> Jurisdictional Exception Rule
> Supplemental Standards Rule
> Definitions

Preamble

Webster defines the word "preamble" as "an introduction to a statute stating its reason and purpose; preliminary." The Preamble to the USPAP does, indeed, state its reason and purpose as reflected in the first paragraph of the Preamble:

> The *purpose* of these Standards is to establish requirements for *professional appraisal practice*, which includes appraisal, consulting, and review, as defined. The intent of these Standards is to *promote and maintain* a high level of *public trust* in *professional appraisal practice*.

The Preamble makes it quite clear that the uniform standards are for appraisers and the users of appraisal services. Furthermore, the appraiser assumes liability to each intended user of the appraiser's services. Also of interest in the Preamble is the reference to a "professional appraisal practice." Implicit in the wording is the assumption that the person carrying out the appraisal assignment will do so in a professional manner.

Ethics Rule

The Ethics Rule of the USPAP states in part:

> **To promote and preserve the public trust inherent in professional appraisal practice, an appraiser must observe the highest standards of professional ethics. This Ethics Rule is divided into four sections: Conduct, Management, Confidentiality, and Record Keeping.**

When reading the Ethics Rule, a number of observations can be made. First, and certainly not by accident, the Ethics Rule is the first subsection of this portion of the USPAP. Clearly, the ethical responsibilities of an appraiser are paramount in terms of his or her arriving at and communicating the analyses, opinions and conclusions. Second, this provision assumes the appraiser has a public responsibility as evidenced by the wording:

> **To *promote and preserve* the *public trust inherent* in *professional appraisal practice* . . .**

To be ethical implies that one has personal obligations and responsibilities to someone else and, thus, "looking after number one" means looking after the best interest of your client. Finally, the words "professional appraisal practice" appear in this rule. As will be noted throughout the discussion of the standards, an appraiser is assumed to be a professional and as such is held to a higher level of accountability than would otherwise be expected.

The *Conduct Section* requires the appraiser to perform with impartiality, objectivity and independence. He or she is required to avoid any action that results in communicating assignments in a misleading or fraudulent manner. This includes reliance upon any unproven conclusions. Accordingly, appraisal independence is paramount. Objectivity must be present. To help assume independence, impartiality and objectivity, federal regulatory agencies such as the Federal Deposit Insurance Corporation (FDIC) and the Office of the Comptroller of the Currency (OCC) require that fee appraisers ("appraisers not permanently employed by a given regulated institution") be engaged (hired) by a regulated financial institution or its agent rather than by the borrower. This requirement, as well as the inclusion of a conduct section in the Ethics Rule, is intended to remove any and all doubt as for whom the appraiser works. To further the goal of complete independence, the appraiser always should be employed via a letter of employment (engagement) by the person who employs the appraiser. Furthermore, the agreed-to fee for services rendered always should be paid directly to the appraiser by the person who employs the appraiser even though the appraisal fee may in turn be charged, for example, to the potential borrower as part of the loan application fee(s). Historically, independent contractors, such as fee appraisers, have defined their clients to be: (1) the persons who order the reports and (2) the persons from whom payments are expected. Thus, the understanding as to who is the appraiser's client is made abundantly clear if the client orders the appraisal and pays the appraiser.

Finally, an appraiser must not use or rely on unsupported conclusions relating to characteristics such as race, color, religion, national origin, gender, marital status, familial status, age, receipt of public assistance income, handicap, or an unsupported conclusion that homogeneity of such characteristics is necessary to maximize value. Besides violating the Ethics Rule of the USPAP, such action also violates both federal fair housing and fair lending laws.

The *Management Section* of the Ethics Rule does not permit payment of undisclosed fees, commissions or things of value in connection with the procurement of appraisal services. Furthermore, the acceptance of contingency fees by an appraiser in developing an opinion of value violates the Ethics Rule. This section states:

> **It is unethical for the appraiser to accept compensation for performing an assignment when the assignment results are contingent upon:**
>
> 1. **the reporting of a predetermined result (e.g. opinion of value), or**
> 2. **a direction in value that favors the cause of the client, or**
> 3. **the amount of the value opinion, or**
> 4. **the attainment of a stipulated result, or**
> 5. **the occurrence of a subsequent event directly related to the appraiser's opinions and specific to the assignment's purpose.**

Standards Rule 2-3 requires that as part of the written real property report, the appraiser *must* include a signed certification statement that includes the following acknowledgment:

> **My compensation for completing this assignment is not contingent upon the development or reporting of a predetermined value or direction in value that favors the cause of the client, the amount of the value opinion, the attainment of a stipulated result, or the occurrence of a subsequent event directly related to the intended use of this appraisal.**

False, misleading, or exaggerated advertising also is addressed in the Management Section. An ad that states "See us for an appraisal, we'll make sure you get the loan," violates the Ethics Rule. In addition to advertising, this section also covers the responsibility to an appraiser who works for a firm in which a fellow employee or supervisor may have been the procuring cause of the appraisal assignment. In such an instance, the individual appraiser is responsible to ascertain that there has been no breach of ethics in obtaining, conducting and communicating the appraisal in which he or she is involved.

The *Confidentiality Section* of the Ethics Rule states quite simply:

An appraiser must protect the confidential nature of the appraiser-client relationship.

Again, reference is made to the "appraiser-client relationship." A fiduciary relationship is assumed.

The Confidentiality Section also addresses the use of confidential information; and it recognizes three instances in which the appraiser may have to disclose confidential factual data. There are specific instances cited in the USPAP in which disclosure of confidential information is acceptable. Disclosure can be made to:

1. the client and persons specifically authorized by the client;

2. state enforcement agencies and such third parties as may be authorized by due process of law; and

3. a duly authorized professional peer review committee except when such disclosure to a committee would violate applicable law or regulation .

Examples of the first instance, persons specifically authorized by the client, would include the potential borrower and other financial institutions who may be participating in the loan if the purpose of the appraisal is for loan documentation. State enforcement agencies and parties authorized by due process of law would include, state appraisal licensing/certification boards as well as the results of legal action in which through the rules of discovery the opposing side in a lawsuit has the legal right to review the appraisal report and related documentation. Finally, an example of a professional peer review committee would include, an appraisal organization in which the appraiser is seeking professional membership. A common practice of such organizations is the requirement that the appraiser show samples of his or her work as part of the application for membership process. The Confidentiality Section of the Ethics Rule makes it unethical for a member of such a duly authorized professional peer review committee to disclose confidential information or factual data presented to the committee.

If a client is concerned that information contained in an appraisal report is of such a nature that it should not be disclosed, then the client should include in the employment contract with the appraiser a statement that these appraisals cannot be used to present qualifications to a professional peer review committee without the prior written consent of the client. As a practical matter, appraisal organization review committees are not concerned with or interested in the subject matter of the appraisal assignments they review as a condition of membership or designation. The purpose of reviewing such work is to see if the appraiser has followed the appraisal process and if he or she has incorporated the correct procedure into the assignment. Unless unusual circumstances exist, a client should not be concerned with information contained in an appraisal "going out to everybody" via a professional peer review committee. However, as noted in the comments, "when all confidential elements of confidential information are removed through redaction or the process of aggregation, client authorization is not required for the disclosure of the remaining information, as modified."

The fourth and final section of the Ethics Rule addresses the appraiser's requirements for *Record Keeping.* Appraisers are required to prepare a workfile for each assignment and to retain such workfiles for each assignment for a period of at least:

1.   five (5) years after preparation, or

2.   at least two (2) years after final disposition of any judicial proceeding in which testimony was given,

whatever period expires last. The five-year and/or two-year requirements are minimum. Some states have enacted into their appraisal laws record-keeping provisions greater than the five and/or two years. In such cases, the longer of the two (USPAP or state statute) would prevail. As a practical matter, appraisers often keep their files for a much longer period of time than these minimums require.

Competency Rule

The Competency Rule states:

Prior to accepting an assignment or entering into an agreement to perform any assignment, an appraiser must properly identify the problem to be addressed and have the knowledge and experience to complete the assignment competently; or alternatively:

1.   **disclose the lack of knowledge and/or experience to the client before accepting the assignment; and**

2.   **take all steps necessary or appropriate to complete the assignment competently; and**

3.   **describe the lack of knowledge and/or experience and the steps taken to complete the assignment competently in the report.**

The Competency Rule provides an integral component of the uniform standards. As noted in the comments section, the *background* and *experience* of appraisers varies widely and "a lack of knowledge or experience can lead to inaccurate or inappropriate appraisal practice."

The introductory words of this rule, "prior to accepting an assignment," fully explain its intent. Specifically, the fact that someone is licensed or certified by the state or holds a recognized designation by a national appraisal organization does not in itself mean the individual is automatically qualified or competent to carry out any and all appraisal assignments. Licensing and certification of appraisers have established *minimum* criteria for showing competency. The education, experience and examination requirements that must be fulfilled to satisfy licensing and certification can be met by someone who has experience and knowledge across broad appraisal topics, as well as by someone who has specialized in a particular subarea of real estate valuation/appraisal. To imply that a certified appraiser is competent for any and all appraisal assignments simply by showing that he or she has met minimum state requirements misses the intent of licensing and certification. The burden of proof of competency is on the shoulders of the appraiser in terms of showing knowledge and experience prior to accepting an appraisal assignment. Once that lack of knowledge and/or experience has been properly noted, the appraiser has an obligation to take the steps necessary or appropriate to competently complete the assignment. Such steps certainly would include consultation with persons who have knowledge and experience with the type of appraisal problem to be addressed in the assignment. For example, an appraiser may not possess the expertise necessary to address environmental issues, structural problems, or architectural design components. However, because the Competency Rule is specifically included in the uniform standards, every appraiser should be expected to know when he or she should seek help. Anything less is a violation of this rule of the standards.

A question that arises in regard to this rule concerns the situation when the appraiser believes he or she is competent prior to taking the assignment. During the course of collecting and analyzing data information may be uncovered that leads the appraiser to question his or her own competency. In certain circumstances, there is obviously no way an appraiser would know if he or she has the experience and knowledge necessary to complete the assignment until certain steps in the appraisal process have been completed. The Competency Rule specifically addresses what the appraiser must do if such is the case. At this point, the appraiser is obligated to notify the client and then follow steps 2 and 3, specifically: (2) take all steps necessary or appropriate to complete the assignment competently and (3) describe the lack of knowledge and/or experience and the steps taken to complete the assignment competently in the report.

The Competency Rule also addresses the common situation in which an appraiser, competent in terms of experience, is asked to travel to geographic areas where he or she has not conducted appraisal work. This could occur when a financial institution desires to lend money on property in geographic areas other than where the financial institution is located. In such an instance, the institution is comfortable with and confident in the appraisal work of an individual who has been employed by the institution, so this particular appraiser is requested to complete the assignment in the new geographic area. In such an event, the Competency Rule requires the appraiser to spend whatever time is necessary to become familiar with the local market, specifically to understand the demand-and-supply components relating to the market. If the appraiser cannot devote the time necessary to become familiar with the local market, then he or she should affiliate with a local appraiser who is qualified to render opinions in regard to the local market. This action should help ensure the completion of a competent appraisal report. The importance of an appraiser associating with someone who understands the local market is further evidenced by the following statement in the Competency Rule: "The necessary understanding of local market conditions provides the bridge between a sale and a comparable sale or a rental and a comparable rental." The intent of this statement is to stress the importance to an appraiser of taking the steps necessary to ensure confidence in the conclusions, analyses and opinions expressed when one is asked to travel to locations outside the geographic area of expertise. Most appraisers can identify sales or rentals. Not everyone, however, can identify a comparable sale or a comparable rental. Competency also applies to other factors such as specific markets and analytical methods.

Departure Rule

The Departure Rule of the USPAP states in part:

> **This rule permits exceptions from sections of the Uniform Standards that are classified as specific requirements rather than binding requirements. The burden of proof is on the appraiser to decide before accepting an assignment and invoking this rule that the scope of work applied will result in opinions or conclusions that are credible. The burden of disclosure is also on the appraiser to report any departures from specific requirements.**

The Departure Rule, specifically why it was included as part of the uniform standards and how the financial institution regulatory agencies initially responded, has caused a great deal of confusion and misinformation. Before addressing the question of how members of the Appraisal Subcommittee originally addressed recognition of the Departure Rule, let us examine why such a rule is included and what the intent of the USPAP is for providing a departure.

Binding Requirements Versus Specific Requirements. As noted in the Preamble to the USPAP, "The standards contain binding requirements as well as specific requirements to which the Departure Rule may apply under certain conditions." Furthermore, an examination of any of the standards rules in Standards 1 - 3 reveals that some of the standards rules are followed by the statement: "This Standards Rule contains binding requirements from which departure is not permitted," while other standards rules are followed by the statement: "This Standards Rule contains specific requirements from which departure is permitted." Clearly the intent, as evidenced in the wording contained in the Preamble, is to allow some flexibility on the part of the appraiser if and when the appraiser enters into an agreement to perform an assignment calling for something less than would be expected in a complete appraisal.

As evidenced by the wording in the Departure Rule, the burden of proof is squarely on the shoulders of the appraiser to determine when departure is acceptable:

> **An appraiser may enter into an agreement to perform an assignment in which the scope of work is less than, or different from, the work that would otherwise be required by the specific requirements, provided that prior to entering into such an agreement:**

> 1. **the appraiser has determined that the appraisal or consulting process to be performed is not so limited that the results of the assignment are no longer credible;**

> 2. **the appraiser has advised the client that the assignment calls for something less than, or different from, the work required by the specific requirements and that the report will clearly identify and explain the departure(s); and**

3.   **the client has agreed that the performance of a limited appraisal or consulting service would be appropriate, given the intended use.**

In addition to advising the client that the appraisal assignment calls for something less than or different from the work required by the specific requirements, the Departure Rule requires that prior to invoking the Departure Rule, the client "has agreed that the performance of a limited appraisal or consulting service would be appropriate given the intended use." This requirement of client agreement indicates the intentions of the USPAP for inclusion of the client in the decision as to the extent of the assignment, the scope of work undertaken and the intent of the appraiser in completing the assignment.

Certain Standards Rules do not permit departure, particularly as the USPAP relates to the appraisal of real property. S.R.1-1, S.R. 1-2, S.R.1-5, S.R.2-1, S.R. 2-2, and S.R.2-3 do not permit departure. Each of these standards rules are followed by the comment "This Standards Rule contains binding requirement from which departure is not permitted."

As noted earlier, when FIRREA was enacted, the financial institution regulatory agencies were given the responsibility to adopt final rules, if the agencies determined that such additional standards would be required in order to properly carry out the agencies' statutory responsibilities. Accordingly, the members of the Appraisal Subcommittee originally required conformity with USPAP "except that the Departure Provision (Rule) of the USPAP shall not apply to federally related transactions." In the opinion of the members of the Appraisal Subcommittee, the Departure Rule would allow an appraisal to be performed that could be entirely different from an "appraisal" as intended in Title XI of FIRREA. However, since the adoption of the original, final appraisal rules by the regulatory agencies, amendments have been made, and today, the financial institution regulatory agencies as well as other users of appraisal services do recognize the Departure Rule.

If an appraiser enters into an agreement to perform an appraisal or consulting service calling for something less than would be required if the appraiser followed the specific requirements, then the appraisal report must clearly identify and explain the departure(s) and the impact, if any, that the departure has on the analyses, opinions and conclusions of the appraiser. The appraiser must disclose any departures from specific requirements. Not all specific requirements are applicable to every assignment. When a specific requirement is not *applicable* to a given assignment, the specific requirement is irrelevant and therefore no departure is needed. However, when a specific requirement is *necessary* to a given assignment, departure is *not* permitted.

Jurisdictional Exception Rule

The Jurisdictional Exception Rule states:

If any part of these standards is contrary to the law or public policy of any jurisdiction, only that part shall be void and of no force or effect in that jurisdiction.

While the USPAP has become recognized as the national appraisal standards, this exception in the USPAP notes the existence of state (jurisdictional) statutes, as well as case law. For example, in some jurisdictions, a definition of market value exists in the state constitution. Thus, if an appraisal is being performed in one of those states, reference would be made to the definition that exists in that jurisdiction. Such an occurrence would be especially common in eminent domain appraisal assignments where, for the purpose of taking land for public use, the state constitution or the state supreme court has a definition different from one included in the USPAP. Likewise, certain states have enacted record keeping requirements in their appraisal statutes that necessitate the keeping of records for a longer period of time than is required by the USPAP.

Supplemental Standards Rule

This rule states:

These Uniform Standards provide the common basis for all appraisal practice. Supplemental standards applicable to appraisals prepared for specific purposes or property types may be issued(i.e. published) by public agencies and other entities that establish public policy. An appraiser and client must ascertain whether any such published supplemental standards in addition to these Uniform Standards apply to the assignment being considered.

The purpose of this provision is quite clear. As noted, the USPAP provides the common basis for all appraisal practices. The intent of this rule is to set a broad framework within which appraisal, review and consulting will function. An important point in this Supplemental Standards Rule concerns the burden placed on both the appraiser and client. As noted, "An appraiser and client must ascertain whether any supplemental standards in addition to these Uniform Standards apply to the assignment being considered." Because the final rules of the regulatory agencies require the financial institution to be the client, a financial institution has an obligation to the appraiser to keep him or her informed as to what requirements must be met. In addition, public agencies such as state highway departments have published written supplemental standards. Any appraiser under contract with a local, state or federal agency should have a copy of the appropriate supplemental standards and incorporate the requirements of the standards in the work product. Failure to do so would result in a misleading appraisal which is a violation of the Ethics Rule.

Definitions

The last provision of the Preamble and Rules Section defines various terms commonly used in the appraisal of property, both real and personal. While somewhat "boilerplate," these definitions have become the commonly accepted definitions. Prior to the establishment of the USPAP and its adoption by the major appraisal organizations in the United States, there was no common reference source for the definitions of terms. By including basic definitions in the USPAP, the profession now has a set of terms that have become accepted in the marketplace. As the uniform standards have become more widely accepted, more definitions have been added. In addition, some state appraisal boards have adopted numerous definitions by statute. These definitions also should be studied and incorporated into the appraiser's work product.

In recent editions of the USPAP, a number of words are defined in the Glossary which is not an integral part of the USPAP as is the Definitions Section. The Glossary is a form of "other communication" the Appraisal Standards Board is authorized to issue. Even though market value is not defined in the Definitions Section, but rather explained, the term should be studied and understood by appraisers since, in most real property appraisal assignments, the purpose of the assignment is to render an opinion as to the market value of the real property.

The Glossary defines market value as:

The most probable price which a property should bring in a competitive and open market under all conditions requisite to a fair sale, the buyer and seller each acting prudently and knowledgeably, and assuming the price is not affected by undue stimulus. Implicit in this definition is the consummation of a sale as of a specified date and the passing of title from seller to buyer under conditions whereby:

3. buyer and seller are typically motivated;
4. both parties are well informed or well advised, and acting in what they consider their best interests;
5. a reasonable time is allowed for exposure in the open market;
6. payment is made in terms of cash in United States dollars or in terms of financial arrangements comparable thereto; and
7. the price represents the normal consideration for the property sold unaffected by special or creative financing or sales concessions granted by anyone associated with the sale.

Preamble and Rules—Key Points

- The Preamble and Rules Section sets the general tone for the responsibilities of an appraiser.

- The Preamble recognizes the professional appraiser and his or her obligations to the users of appraisal services.

- Public trust is inherent in a professional appraisal practice.

- The Ethics Rule is divided into four specific sections: conduct, management, confidentiality, and record keeping.

- The acceptance of a contingency fee by an appraiser when developing an opinion of value is unethical.

- False, misleading, or exaggerated advertising violates the Management Section of the Ethics Rule.

- An appraiser must protect the confidential nature of the appraiser-client relationship.

- Appraisers are required to retain their workfiles for a period of at least five (5) years after preparation or at least two (2) years after final disposition of any judicial proceeding in which testimony was given, whichever period expires last.

- Prior to accepting an appraisal assignment, an appraiser must have the knowledge and experience necessary to complete the assignment competently, or else take the specific steps to properly serve the client's best interest.

- The USPAP permits an appraiser to accept a limited assignment; the appraiser, however, must determine that the results will not be confusing or misleading.

- The fact that a part or a portion of the USPAP is contrary to law or public policy in a specific jurisdiction does not void the remaining parts or portions of the uniform standards.

- Appraisers must ascertain whether any supplemental standards in addition to the USPAP apply to the assignment being considered.

- The USPAP contains definitions of key terms commonly used in appraisal assignments.

Review Questions

1. According to the Preamble, which of the following statements is correct?

   A. The standards are for appraisers and all readers of appraisal reports.
   B. The USPAP reflects the current standards of the appraisal profession.
   C. The standards contain binding requirements to which a Departure Rule must apply under all conditions.
   D. The intent of the USPAP is to assist appraisers in setting appraisal fees.

2. An appraiser is employed by a national company for the purpose of estimating the market value of a hotel that is being reassessed for property tax purposes. He completed the report on June 30, 2000. On September 22, 2001, he testified in court on behalf of the owner who has appealed the tax assessment. The court ruled in favor of the owner with final disposition occurring December 1, 2001. At a minimum, the appraiser must keep his records until

   A. June 30, 2002.
   B. December 1, 2003.
   C. June 30, 2005.
   D. December 1, 2006.

3. The requirement that the appraiser must have the knowledge and experience to complete the assignment is part of which rule of the USPAP?

   A. Competency Rule
   B. Ethics Rule
   C. Departure Rule
   D. Conduct Rule

4. According to the definitions in the USPAP, "a study of the cost-benefit relationship of an economic endeavor" is referred to as a(n)

   A. cash flow analysis.
   B. feasibility analysis.
   C. investment analysis.
   D. market analysis.

5. If an appraiser enters into an agreement to perform an appraisal service that calls for something less than would be required by the specific appraisal requirements of the USPAP, then the appraiser must

   A. clearly set forth this fact in the report.
   B. have another appraiser cosign the report.
   C. accept hourly compensation rather than a flat fee.
   D. not refer to the report as an appraisal.

6. As per the definitions in the USPAP, "the party or parties who engages an appraiser in a specific assignment" is the

   A. client.
   B. customer.
   C. intermediary.
   D. cosigner.

7. According to the Ethics Rule which of the following statements is correct?

   A. Whenever an appraiser develops an opinion of value, acceptance of compensation contingent on the reporting of a predetermined value is ethical.
   B. When an opinion of value is necessary as part of an appraisal consulting assignment, contingent compensation is permitted.
   C. To promote and preserve the public trust inherent in professional appraisal practice, an appraiser must observe the highest standards of professional ethics.
   D. An appraiser can, without violation of the USPAP, communicate assignment results in a misleading or fraudulent manner.

8. That which is contrary to what exists, but is supposed for the purpose of analysis is known as a(an):

   A. extraordinary assumption
   B. extraordinary condition
   C. hypothetical condition
   D. hypothetical assumption

9. At a minimum, how long must an appraiser retain his or her workfile after preparation of the appraisal report?

    A. No minimum time is set
    B. One year
    C. Two years
    D. Five years

10. In regard to the Departure Rule, which of the following statements is correct?

    A. This rule does not permit exceptions to sections of the USPAP.
    B. The burden of proof is on the user of the appraisal report to decide that the scope of work applied will result in opinions or conclusions that are credible.
    C. The Departure Rule extends to all the standards rules of the USPAP.
    D. The burden of disclosure is on the appraiser to report any departures from specific requirements.

11. The disclosure of confidential factual data obtained from a client to certain individuals is permitted under the Ethics Rule. Certain individuals include

    A. persons specifically authorized by the client.
    B. all certified appraisers.
    C. any previous owner of the property.
    D. members of an appraisal organization of which the appraiser is a member.

12. The "interests, benefits, and rights inherent in the ownership of real estate" is the normal definition for which of the following terms?

    A. Real estate
    B. Real property
    C. Personal property
    D. Fixtures

13. According to the definitions of the USPAP, a "report" includes which of the following means of communication?

    A. Oral communication only
    B. Written communication only
    C. Oral or written communication
    D. The USPAP does not define a report

14.   The Ethics Rule is divided into four sections. Which of the following activities is one of those four sections?

   A.   Departure
   B.   Jurisdictional Exception
   C.   Record Keeping
   D.   Competency

15.   Which of the following persons (entities) is specifically mentioned as someone to whom an appraiser may disclose confidential factual data obtained from a client?

   A   Any reader of the appraisal report
   B   State enforcement agencies and such third parties as may be authorized by due process of law
   C.   Appraisers who have previously rendered an opinion of value on the subject property
   D.   Prior owners of the appraised property

16.   Based on the provisions of the Supplemental Standards Rule, which of the following statements is correct?

   A.   The USPAP provides the common basis for all appraisal practice.
   B.   Supplemental standards must be issued by any public agency in which public funds are involved.
   C.   Appraisers and clients must ascertain whether supplemental standards apply to the appraisal assignment.
   D.   Certain client groups must issue supplemental standards.

Standard 1

REAL PROPERTY APPRAISAL, DEVELOPMENT

Standard 1 states:

In developing a real property appraisal, an appraiser must identify the problem to be solved and the scope of work necessary to solve the problem, and correctly complete research and analysis necessary to produce a credible appraisal.

Standard 1 is directed toward the substantive aspect of developing a competent appraisal of real property. In short, this standard follows the appraisal process, the systematic step-by-step approach that should be used by an appraiser in all real property appraisal assignments. Standard 1 contains five standards rules, three of which are binding requirements and two of which are specific requirements. As can be seen in Figure 1, the appraisal process begins with the definition of the problem, proceeds through the necessary appraisal steps, and culminates in the preparation of the appraisal report. Standard 1 covers the process down through reconciliation and final value estimate. Report preparation, the last step in the appraisal process, is the subject of Standard 2.

While the appraisal process is the same regardless of the appraisal assignment, the specifics within each of the steps will vary from one appraisal assignment to another. For example, application of the income approach may not be appropriate in the appraisal of a single-family residence. An assignment seeking the replacement cost for insurance purposes probably does not require an analysis of highest and best use. Thus, while the appraisal process should be followed in all assignments, the *judgment* of the appraiser as well as his or her *knowledge* and *experience* will be called on to correctly lead the appraiser through the process. Appraising is not a science; therefore, it would stand to reason that the appraisal standard that mirrors the appraisal process would include both specific and binding requirements for the appraiser. Operative words such as "develop," "identify," and "when applicable" appear throughout Standard 1. The burden clearly is on the appraiser to determine when he or she must develop, identify, or apply. The appraiser must determine the scope of work necessary to complete the appraisal assignment competently.

Figure 1

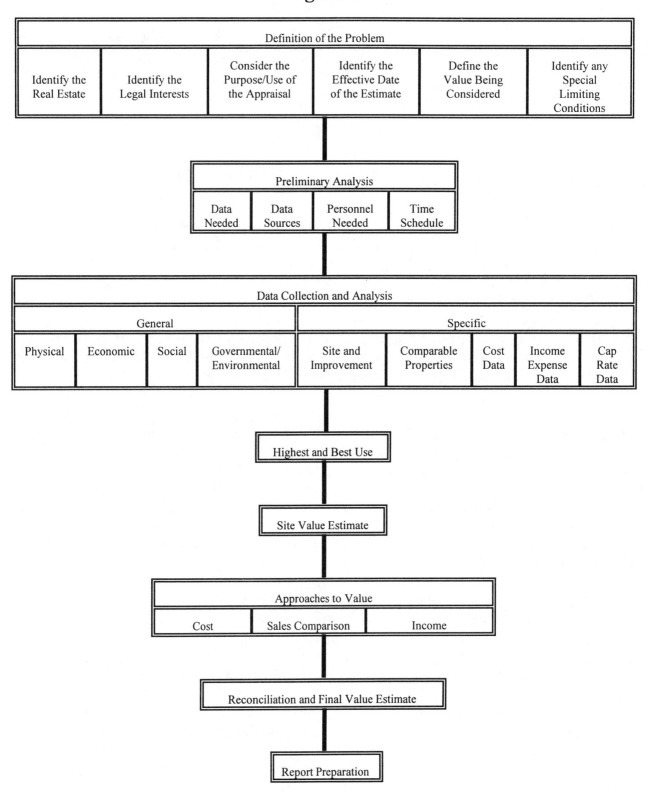

Two types of appraisals are permitted under Standard 1:

Complete Appraisal : The act or process of developing an opinion of value or an opinion of value developed without invoking the Departure Rule; and

Limited Appraisal : The act or process of developing an opinion of value or an opinion of value developed under and resulting from invoking the Departure Rule.

Appraisers should have the knowledge and experience (see Competency Rule) necessary to identify when a limited appraisal is appropriate. If after consultation and agreement with the client that something less than a complete appraisal would be appropriate and would not be misleading, given the intended use, the appraiser can invoke the Departure Rule and the appraisal can be accepted and performed.

Quite often, the client who requests a limited appraisal is a frequent user of appraisals performed by the appraiser, as well as someone who understands market conditions and how the appraisal will be used. The appraiser is responsible for knowing the level of understanding that the client has and should take the steps necessary to document that the client has agreed to a limited appraisal (see Departure Rule). For example, a financial institution may have a large home equity loan business and relies on minimum market and property information prior to making such loans. The dollar amounts loaned may be such, for example under $50,000, and the loan-to-value ratio may be such, always less than 50 percent, that the lender is comfortable with limited appraisals which only utilize the sales comparison approach. In such cases, the appraiser and lender (client) could agree that a limited appraisal is both appropriate and acceptable.

Limited appraisal assignments encompass numerous nomenclatures developed by both appraisers and clients. An understanding of this terminology has become increasingly important in light of action by the financial institution regulatory agencies in the mid 1990s in regard to raising the de minimis level (a dollar loan amount below which an appraisal is not required). Among the terms currently used to denote different types of limited appraisals are the following:

Evaluation - a term frequently used by financial institutions to denote the opinion of value needed when the amount of the transaction is less than the de minimus level requiring an appraisal. Typically for single-family residential real estate, the collection, verification, and analysis of data is limited to the sales comparison approach. Clearly, when an appraiser accepts an assignment to perform an evaluation considering only one of the approaches to value, the assignment becomes a limited appraisal.

Update of an Appraisal - an extension of an original appraisal. The original appraisal could have been either a limited appraisal or a complete appraisal which was relied upon by the client for a prior business decision. An update changes the effective date of the value opinion and would be used only after an original appraisal report had been completed; therefore, the person(s) who receives the update already will have had in his or her possession and file the original appraisal report. As per the advice given in Advisory Opinion 3 (AO-3), three conditions should be met *before* an update assignment is accepted:

1.   The original appraiser's firm and client are involved;

2.   The real estate has undergone no significant change since the original appraisal; and

3.   The time period between the effective date of the original appraisal (or most recent update) and the effective date of the pending update is not unreasonably long for the type of real estate involved.

Recertification of Value - a limited appraisal performed for the purpose of confirming whether or not the completed improvements and/or market conditions are consistent with the assumptions and statements made in an earlier prospective appraisal. For example, a recertification would be undertaken to verify if the completed property was built as per the plans and specifications used to initially estimate the value. Under a recertification of value, the effective date of the value opinion does not change.

As will be noted in the discussion of Standard 2, the reliability of either a complete appraisal or a limited appraisal is not affected by the type of appraisal report prepared. Rather, the reliability is based on the extent of the scope of work performed by the appraiser.

The five standards rules are as follows:

Standards Rule 1-1 (Binding Requirement)

In developing a real property appraisal, an appraiser must:

(a)   be aware of, understand, and correctly employ those recognized methods and techniques that are necessary to produce a credible appraisal;

(b)   not commit a substantial error of omission or commission that significantly affects an appraisal;

(c)   not render appraisal services in a careless or negligent manner, such as by making a series of errors that, although considered individually, may not significantly affect the results of an appraisal, in the aggregate affect the credibility of those results.

Standards Rule 1-1 sets the tone for Standard 1 and as such it is a binding requirement. As would be expected, this standards rule is somewhat broad in scope. Standards Rule 1-1 calls attention to the need to follow recognized methods and techniques. In addition, the appraiser should stay current and continuously improve his or her skills. An attitude of "I've been doing it that way for twenty years" may not be sufficient to show proficiency. This rule addresses the competency that is necessary by anyone undertaking an appraisal assignment. Due diligence and due care are required.

Standards Rule 1-2 (Binding Requirement)

In developing a real property appraisal, an appraiser must:

(a)   identify the client and other intended users;

(b)   identify the intended use of the appraiser's opinions and conclusions;

(c)   identify the purpose of the assignment, including the type and definition of value to be developed; and, if the value opinion to be developed is market value, ascertain whether the value is to be the most probable price:
   (i)   in terms of cash; or
   (ii)   in terms of financial arrangements equivalent to cash; or
   (iii) in other precisely defined terms; and
   (iv)   if the opinion of value is to be based on non-market financing or financing with unusual conditions or incentives, the terms of such financing must be clearly identified and the appraiser's opinion of their contributions to or negative influence on value must be developed by analysis of relevant market data.

(d)   identify the effective date of the appraiser's opinions and conclusions;

(e)   identify the characteristics of the property that are relevant to the purpose and intended use of the appraisal, including:
   (i)   its location and physical, legal, and economic attributes;
   (ii)   the real property interest to be valued;
   (iii) any personal property, trade fixtures or intangible items that are not real property but are included in the appraisal;
   (iv)   any known easements, restrictions, encumbrances, leases, reservations, covenants, contracts, declarations, special assessments, ordinances, or other items of a similar nature;
   (v)   whether the subject property is a fractional interest, physical segment, or partial holding.

(f)   identify the scope of work necessary to complete the assignment:

(g)   identify any extraordinary assumptions necessary in the assignment;

(h)   identify any hypothetical conditions necessary in the assignment.

Standards Rule 1-2 is also a binding requirement. Broadly speaking, this standards rule covers the initial step in the appraisal process that is the definition of the problem. While the first step in the appraisal process and the requirements covered by Standards Rule 1-2 may seem somewhat "boilerplate," the specifics of this first step will vary from assignment to assignment. The value being considered will not be the same in all appraisal assignments. Even if the opinion of value is market value, a Jurisdictional Exception Rule may result in a definition different from that contained in the Glossary to the USPAP.

Close attention should be called to Standards Rule 1-2(e). This binding requirement requires the appraiser to recognize that certain items, such as personal property or trade fixtures, are not part of real property and thus should not be included in an overall value opinion of the real estate. The presence of such items as machinery and equipment may require expertise beyond that of the real estate appraiser. Remember, the Competency Rule states "prior to accepting an assignment. . . an appraiser must have the knowledge and experience. . . ." If the knowledge and experience are not present, the appraiser must disclose that shortcoming to the client and take the necessary steps to correct the deficiency. One step commonly taken is to employ the services of someone competent to render an opinion of the value of such items or components.

Finally, this standard requires the appraiser to identify the scope of work necessary to complete the assignment. Scope of work encompasses the amount and type of information researched and the analysis applied in an assignment. Any extraordinary assumptions and/or hypothetical conditions necessary in the assignment must also be identified.

Standards Rule 1-3 (Specific Requirement)

When the value opinion to be developed is market value, and given the scope of work identified in accordance with Standards Rule 1-2(f), an appraiser must:

(a)   identify and analyze the effect on use and value of existing land use regulations, reasonably probable modifications of such land use regulations, economic demand, the physical adaptability of the real estate, and market area trends;

(b)   develop an opinion of the highest and best use of the real estate.

Standards Rule 1-3 is not a binding requirement. When the value opinion is market value, this standards rule addresses the need for the appraiser to include land use regulations, economic trends, market area trends and, specifically, highest and best use analysis. The appraiser is cautioned against "making an unsupported assumption or premise about market area trend, effective age, and remaining life."

In many appraisal assignments, the opinion of value to be given is market value and, thus, a highest and best use analysis (and statement) is both appropriate and necessary. All real estate appraisers should have a clear understanding of highest and best use, the four "tests" normally applied and the rationale for valuing the site as if vacant and available for its highest and best use.

Standards Rule 1-4 (Specific Requirement)

In developing a real property appraisal, an appraiser must collect, verify, and analyze all information pertinent to the appraisal problem, given the scope of work identified in accordance with Standards Rule 1-2(f).

(a)   When a sales comparison approach is applicable, an appraiser must analyze such comparable sales data, as are available to indicate a value conclusion.

(b)   When a cost approach approach is applicable, an appraiser must:
   (i)   develop an opinion of site value by an appropriate appraisal method or technique;
   (ii)   analyze such comparable cost data as are available to estimate the cost new of the improvements(if any);

   (iii)   analyze such comparable data as are available to estimate the difference between cost new and the present worth of the improvements (accrued depreciation).

(c)   When an income approach to value is applicable, an appraiser must:
   (i)   analyze such comparable rental data as are available to estimate the market rental of the property;
   (ii)   analyze such comparable operating expense data as are available to estimate the operating expenses of the property;
   (iii)   analyze such comparable data as are available to estimate rates of capitalization and/or rates of discount; and
   (iv)   base projections of future rent and expenses on reasonably clear and appropriate evidence.

(d)   When developing an opinion of the value of a leased fee estate or a leasehold estate, an appraiser must analyze the effect on value, if any, of the terms and conditions of the lease(s).

(e)   An appraiser must analyze the effect on value, if any, of the assemblage of the various estates or component parts of a property and refrain from valuing the whole solely by adding together the individual values of the various estates or component parts.

(f)   An appraiser must analyze the effect on value, if any, of anticipated public or private improvements, located on or off the site, to the extent that market actions reflect such anticipated improvements as of the effective appraisal date.

(g)   An appraiser must analyze the effect on value of any personal property, trade fixtures or intangible items that are not real property but are included in the appraisal.

(h) **When appraising proposed improvements, an appraiser must examine and have available for future examination:**

    (i) **plans, specifications, or other documentation sufficient to identify the scope and character of the proposed improvements;**

    (ii) **evidence indicating the probable time of completion of the proposed improvements; and**

    (iii) **reasonably clear and appropriate evidence supporting development costs, anticipated earnings, occupancy projections, and the anticipated competition at the time of completion.**

Standards Rule 1-4 is not a binding requirement; rather, it is a specific requirement and addresses primarily the "traditional" approaches to value. Specifically, the appraiser is to value the site and the improvements by the appropriate method(s). Proper techniques for site valuation, while seemingly simple, can be both complicated and difficult to perform. All appraisers are advised to carefully review the acceptable site valuation techniques before deciding which technique(s) to use in a particular assignment. In regard to the traditional approaches to value, the appraiser is advised to "analyze . . . such comparable sales data. . . such comparable cost data. . . such comparable rental/expense/cap rate data" as necessary and appropriate. The appraiser is expected to know when and how each of the recognized approaches to value is applicable and/or necessary to the specific appraisal assignment. The corresponding reporting requirement, "explain and support the exclusion of any of the usual valuation approaches," is addressed in Standards Rule 2-2(a)(b)(c)(xi).

The importance of examining plans, specifications, or other documentation if the appraisal assignment involves proposed improvements also is addressed in Standards Rule 1-4. As noted in one of the comments sections of this standards rule, the appraisal of proposed improvements may require a complete feasibility analysis, which is addressed in Standards Rule 4-6, Real Property/Real Estate Consulting, Development.

Standards Rule 1-5 (Binding Requirement)

In developing a real property appraisal, an appraiser must:

(a) **analyze any current Agreement of Sale, option, or listing of the property, if such information is available to the appraiser in the normal course of business;**

(b) **analyze any prior sales of the property that occurred within the following minimum time periods:**

    (i) **one year for one-to-four family residential property; and**

    (ii) **three years for all other property types;**

(c) **reconcile the quality and quantity of data available and analyzed within the approaches used and the applicability or suitability of the approaches used.**

Standards Rule 1-5 requires the appraiser to examine current information, such as leases, options and agreements of sale of the subject property, if such information is available to the appraiser in the *normal* course of business. This binding requirement is no doubt included as a response to the problems that arise when a real estate appraisers is accused of rendering an opinion of value on property without properly analyzing the circumstances surrounding the leasing and prior sales of such property. Specifically, what types of concessions were made to tenants? What was/is the creditworthiness of those tenants? Was the prior sale simply a "land flip" intended to create the illusion of a value increase in the subject property to justify a higher value for loan purposes? Standards Rule 1-5 requires the appraiser to consider and analyze any prior sales of the subject property that have occurred within:

(i)   one year for one-to-four family residential property; and

(ii)   three years for all other property types.

Both of these time frames are *minimums*. The appraiser may find it beneficial to examine prior sales of the subject property over a much longer period of time than the one-year and three-year periods.

Standard 1—Key Points

▸   Standard 1 addresses the development of a real property appraisal.

▸   The standard mirrors the appraisal process.

▸   Standard 1 permits two types of appraisals: complete and limited.

▸   The reliability of an appraisal is based on the extent of the appraisal process performed by the appraiser.

▸   The topics covered can be used as a convenient "checklist" by both appraisers and clients of appraisal services.

▸   Three of the five standards rules are binding requirements.

▸   Standard 1 recognizes that perfection is impossible to attain and competence does not require perfection.

▸   Valuation of personal property or business appraisal may require additional expertise.

▸   When applicable, the appraiser must value the site by an appropriate method or technique.

▸   Highest and best use should be addressed to the extent that is required for a proper solution of the appraisal problem being considered.

▸ The appraiser must analyze the data needed for the three approaches to value if the appraiser deems the approach(es) to be applicable and necessary.

▸ The appraiser should weigh historical information and trends.

▸ Proposed improvements should be appraised only after examining plans, specifications, or other documentation.

▸ An appraiser must examine prior agreements of sale, options, or listings if such information is available in the normal course of business.

▸ The minimum time frames for examining sales/listing information is one year for one-to-four residential property and three years for all other property types.

Review Questions

1. Which of the following actions of Standard 1 is a specific requirement?

   A. Identify the client and other intended users of the real property appraisal
   B. Define the value being developed
   C. Identify the effective date of the appraiser's opinions and conclusions
   D. If a leasehold interest is involved, also value the whole as if were fee simple

2. According to the USPAP, which of the following binding requirements is a part of Standard 1?

   A. The appraiser must not commit a substantial error of omission or commission that significantly affects an appraisal.
   B. When applicable, the site must always be valued by at least three methods or techniques.
   C. If income-producing property is being appraised, then all three of the traditional approaches to value must be used and explained.
   D. The value being developed must be defined as market value.

3. Standard 1 requires an appraiser to consider and analyze certain legal instruments dealing with the subject property, if such instruments are available through the normal course of business. Which of the following documents is specifically mentioned as one to be considered and analyzed?

   A. Agreement of sale
   B. Promissory note
   C. Deed of trust
   D. Installment sales contract

4. Which of the following actions on the part of the appraiser is a requirement according to Standard 1?

    A. Identify the intended use of the appraiser's opinions and conclusions
    B. Appraise easements, encumbrances, or other items of a similar nature
    C. Copy and include in the report the terms and conditions of the lease(s)
    D. Certify that the appraisal report was prepared in conformity with the USPAP

5. According to the USPAP, which one of the following requirements is part of Standard 1?

    A. The appraiser must not render appraisal services in a careless or negligent manner.
    B. Prior to accepting an appraisal assignment, the appraiser must possess the knowledge and experience necessary to complete the assignment or take specific alternatives.
    C. The appraiser must protect the confidential nature of the appraiser-client relationship.
    D. The appraisal report must contain sufficient information to enable the person(s) who receive or rely on the report to understand it properly.

6. An appraiser must consider and analyze any prior sales for _____ year(s) for one-to-four family residential property and _____ year(s) for all other property types, if such information is available to the appraiser through the normal course of business.

    A. one year; one year
    B. one year; three years
    C. three years; three years
    D. five years; five years

7. Which of the following statements is correct in regard to Standard 1 as it relates to the production of a credible appraisal?

    A. Changes in the development field have little impact on the appraisal profession.
    B. Social changes have no effect on appraisal theory and practice.
    C. Each appraiser must continuously improve his or her skills.
    D. In order to show proficiency, each appraiser must have, as a minimum, ten hours of continuing education each year.

8. According to the USPAP, which of the following statements is an important part of Standard 1?

    A. The appraisal must contain sufficient information to enable the person(s) who receives the report to understand it properly.

    B. The appraiser must not render appraisal services in a careless or negligent manner.

    C. The appraiser must recognize that land is appraised as though vacant for development to its interim use.

    D. For every appraisal assignment, projections of future rent expenses must be based on reasonably clear and appropriate evidence.

9. Which of the following actions is a requirement of Standard 1?

    A. Develop an opinion of site value by the land residual method

    B. Always analyze the effect on value of all possible public or private improvements

    C. State the name(s) of anyone providing significant professional assistance to the person signing the report

    D. Base projections of future rent and expenses on reasonably clear and appropriate evidence

10. Standard 1 contains numerous binding and specific requirements. Which of the following actions is a requirement of Standard 1?

    A. Certify that the compensation received is not based on the reporting of a predetermined value

    B. Analyze, without any exceptions, any current agreements of sale

    C. Appraise proposed improvements only after examining and having available for future examination plans, specs, or other documentation sufficient to identify the scope and character of the proposed improvements

    D. Recognize that land is appraised as though vacant and available for development to its current use

11. In regard to Standard 1, which of the following statements is correct?

    A. Standard 1 is directed toward the substantive aspects of reporting a competent appraisal.

    B. Standard 1 mirrors the appraisal report in the order of topics addressed.

    C. Standard 1 can be used by appraisers and clients as a convenient checklist.

    D. All of the standards rules in Standard 1 are binding requirements.

12.　Which of the following actions on the part of the appraiser is a specific requirement according to Standard 1?

　　A.　Identify the effective date of the appraiser's opinions and conclusions
　　B.　Value the property under its highest and best use
　　C.　Define the value being considered
　　D.　Identify the effect on value of any personal property included in the appraisal

13.　Standard 1 contains numerous requirements. Which of the following actions is a specific requirement of Standard 1?

　　A.　Identify any hypothetical conditions necessary in the assignment
　　B.　Define the value to be developed
　　C.　Consider whether each appraisal technique is applicable
　　D.　Identify the scope of work necessary to complete the assignment

14.　The two types of appraisals permitted to be developed under Standard 1 are

　　A.　full and limited.
　　B.　complete and self-contained.
　　C.　complete and limited.
　　D.　self-contained and summary.

15.　A limited appraisal performed for the purpose of confirming whether or not the completed improvements and/or market conditions are consistent with the assumptions and statements made in an earlier prospective appraisal is commonly referred to as a(n)

　　A.　recertification of value.
　　B.　letter of opinion.
　　C.　update of an appraisal.
　　D.　self-contained evaluation.

Standard 2

REAL PROPERTY APPRAISAL, REPORTING

Standard 2 states:

In reporting the results of a real property appraisal an appraiser must communicate each analysis, opinion, and conclusion in a manner that is not misleading.

Standard 2 is directed toward the content and level of information required in a report. The standard does not dictate the form, format and style of the report. As noted in the Preamble of the USPAP, the appraiser is expected to communicate his or her analyses, opinions and conclusions in a manner that will be meaningful and not misleading to the intended users of the appraiser's services..

The appraiser's intended user does not see nor is he or she part of all the work and effort undertaken by the appraiser during the appraisal process. What the appraiser's intended user does see, however, is the finished product—the appraisal report. Because the purpose of the USPAP is to provide understanding and clarity to the client as well as to other intended users of the report, Standard 2 places significant requirements on the appraiser. Accordingly, three of the four standards rules are binding requirements. Clearly, the intent of these binding requirements is to provide the client and intended users of the appraisal report with minimum information so he or she can clearly understand the appraisal report.

The definitions section of the USPAP identifies three types of written appraisal reports:

Self-Contained Appraisal Report : A written report prepared under Standards Rule 2-2(a) of a Complete or Limited Appraisal performed under STANDARD 1;

Summary Appraisal Report : A written report prepared under Standards Rule 2-2(b) of a Complete or Limited Appraisal performed under STANDARD 1;

Restricted Use Appraisal Report : A written report prepared under Standards Rule 2-2(c) of a Complete or Limited Appraisal performed under STANDARD 1.

As a result of the two types of appraisals (complete and limited) recognized by Standard 1 and the three appraisal reports (self-contained, summary, and restricted use) recognized by Standard 2, there are now six combinations of appraisals and appraisal reports:

APPRAISALS/APPRAISAL REPORT COMBINATIONS

STANDARD 1	STANDARD 2
Complete	Self-contained
Complete	Summary
Complete	Restricted Use
Limited	Self-contained
Limited	Summary
Limited	Restricted Use

Neither the USPAP nor, more specifically, Standard 2 dictates the form, format, or style of the appraisal report. The form, format and/or the style are determined by the needs of the client and intended users and the constraints placed on the appraisal assignment. The reliability of the analyses, opinions and conclusions is not a function of the form, format, or style of the appraisal report; rather, it is a function of the extent to which Standard 1, the appraisal process, is followed.

The appraiser and client must decide which appraisal report option is appropriate for the assignment. Such a decision is part of the first step in the appraisal process, namely the definition of the problem. For a series of appraisal assignments, such as the appraisal of single-family homes for a financial institution, the decision can be that the report option agreed to between the appraiser and the client will cover all of the appraisals. The decision concerning the report option should be specifically mentioned in the engagement letter (or engagement fax) and/or in the appraiser employment contract.

If the appraisal report used is a form report, such as the URAR 1004, then the report option (for example, a complete summary appraisal report) used can appear in the Conditions of Appraisal section of the report (reconciliation section - bottom of page 2). For narrative appraisal reports, the statement as to what report option is being used can be a part of the statement of the purpose and intended use of the appraisal. In addition, the appraiser also may decide to state the report option used in the letter of transmittal as well as in other correspondence with the client and/or intended users.

There are no set rules as to when a self-contained versus a summary appraisal report should be used, if the intended user includes parties other than the client. However, when the intended user does not include parties other than the client, a restricted use appraisal report may be used. The key difference between the three reports involves the level of detail of presentation. Each of the three reports requires a different level of report content and level of information. Specifically, the words *describe* and *summarize* are the operative words that distinguish the self-contained and summary reports.

The four standards rules of Standard 2 are as follows:

Standards Rule 2-1 (Binding Requirement)

Each written or oral real property appraisal report must:

(a) **clearly and accurately set forth the appraisal in a manner that will not be misleading;**

(b) **contain sufficient information to enable the intended users of the appraisal to understand the report properly;**

(c) **clearly and accurately disclose any extraordinary assumption, hypothetical conditions, or limiting condition that directly affects the appraisal and indicate its impact on value.**

As is true with Standards Rule 1-1, Standards Rule 2-1 sets the broad parameters within which the remaining standards rules address specific and binding requirements for properly communicating an appraisal assignment. Standards Rule 2-1 addresses both oral and written appraisal reports. As defined by the uniform standards, a report is "any communication, written or oral, of an appraisal, appraisal review, or consulting service that is transmitted to the client upon completion of an assignment." Clearly, there are instances in which an oral appraisal report is acceptable and, in fact, preferred. For federally related financial transactions, however, oral appraisal reports do not exist, and, in fact, as required under Title XI of FIRREA, all appraisals must be performed in writing. In addition, the published supplemental standards of many regulatory and state agencies require the appraisal report to be in writing.

Standards Rule 2-2 (Binding Requirement) (Editor Note: The words in *italics* denote the differences between the subparts of the three types of appraisal reports).

Each written real property appraisal report must be prepared under one of the following three options and prominently state which option is used: Self-Contained Appraisal Report, Summary Appraisal Report or Restricted Use Appraisal Report.

(a)   **The content of a Self-Contained Appraisal Report must be consistent with the intended use of the appraisal and, at a minimum:**

     (i)   **state the identity of the client *and any intended users*, by name or type;**

     (ii)   **state the intended use of the appraisal;**

     (iii)   ***describe* information sufficient to identify the real estate involved in the appraisal, *including the physical and economic property characteristics relevant to the assignment;***

     (iv)   **state the real property interest appraised;**

     (v)   **state the purpose of the appraisal, including the type *and definition* of value and its source;**

     (vi)   **state the effective date of the appraisal and the date of the report;**

     (vii)   ***describe* sufficient information to disclose to the client and any intended users of the appraisal the scope of work used to develop the appraisal;**

     (viii)   **state all assumptions, hypothetical conditions and limiting conditions that affected the analyses, opinions, and conclusions;**

     (ix)   ***describe* the information analyzed, the appraisal procedures followed, and the reasoning that supports the analyses, opinions, and conclusions;**

     (x)   **state the use of the real estate, existing as of the date of value, and the use of the real estate reflected in the appraisal; and, when the purpose of the assignment is market value, *describe the support and rationale* for the appraiser's opinion of the highest and best use of the real estate;**

     (xi)   **state and explain any permitted departures from specific requirements of STANDARD 1, and the reason for excluding any of the usual valuation approaches;**

     (xii)   **include a signed certification in accordance with Standards Rule 2-3.**

(b) **The content of a Summary Appraisal Report must be consistent with the intended use of the appraisal and, at a minimum:**

 (i) state the identity of the client *and any intended users*, by name or type;

 (ii) state the intended use of the appraisal;

 (iii) *summarize* information sufficient to identify the real estate involved in the appraisal, *including the physical and economic property characteristics relevant to the assignment;*

 (iv) state the real property interest appraised;

 (v) state the purpose of the appraisal, including the type *and definition* of value and its source;

 (vi) state the effective date of the appraisal and the date of the report;

 (vii) *summarize* sufficient information to disclose to the client and any intended users of the appraisal the scope of work used to develop the appraisal;

 (viii) state all assumptions, hypothetical conditions and limiting conditions that affected the analyses, opinions, and conclusions;

 (ix) *summarize* the information analyzed, the appraisal procedures followed, and the reasoning that supports the analyses, opinions, and conclusions;

 (x) state the use of the real estate, existing as of the date of value, and the use of the real estate reflected in the appraisal; and, when the purpose of the assignment is market value, *summarize the support and rationale* for the appraiser's opinion of the highest and best use of the real estate;

 (xi) state and explain any permitted departures from specific requirements of STANDARD 1, and the reason for excluding any of the usual valuation approaches;

 (xii) include a signed certification in accordance with Standards Rule 2-3.

(c) **The content of a Restricted Use Appraisal Report must be consistent with the intended use of the appraisal and, at a minimum:**

 (i) state the identity of the client and by name or type;

 (ii) state the intended use of the appraisal;

(iii)   *state* information sufficient to identify the real estate involved in the appraisal;

(iv)   state the real property interest appraised;

(v)   state the purpose of the appraisal, including the type of value *and refer to the definition of value pertinent to the purpose of the assignment;*

(vi)   state the effective date of the appraisal and the date of the report;

(vii)   *state the extent of the process of collecting, confirming, and reporting data or refer to an assignment agreement retained in the appraiser's workfile, which describes the scope of work to be performed;*

(viii)   state all assumptions, hypothetical conditions and limiting conditions that affect the analyses, opinions, and conclusions;

(ix)   *the workfile;state the appraisal procedures followed, and the value opinion(s) and conclusion(s), and reference*

(x)   *state* the use of the real estate, existing as of the date of value, and the use of the real estate reflected in the appraisal; and, when the purpose of the assignment is market value, *state* the appraiser's opinion of the highest and best use of the real estate;

(xi)   state and explain any permitted departures from specific requirements of **STANDARD 1**; *state the exclusion of any of the usual valuation approaches; and state a prominent use restriction that limits use of the report to the client and warns that the appraiser's opinions and conclusions set forth in the report cannot be understood properly without additional information in the appraiser's workfile;*

(xii)   include a signed certification in accordance with Standards Rule 2-3.

Standards Rule 2-2 is a binding requirement and is intended to include the minimum requirements that must be included in all three types of appraisal reports. The 12 requirements contained in S.R. 2-2(a), S.R. 2-2(b), and S.R. 2-2(c) are very specific, such as the intended use of the appraisal, the definition of the value to be estimated, and the effective date of the appraisal. These 12 minimum requirements should be used as a convenient "checklist" by the appraiser to assure that he or she has included all the content requirements of Standards Rule 2-2.

Self-Contained Appraisal Report - As evidenced by the requirements of S.R. 2-2(a) the self-contained appraisal report should contain all the information significant to solving the defined appraisal problem. Underlying the concept of the self-contained appraisal report is the idea that the reader should expect to find *all* significant data reported in detail; otherwise, the report is not self-contained.

Summary Appraisal Report - As stated in the comment section to S.R. 2-2, "The essential difference among the three options is in the content and the level of information provided." Multiple page discussions in a self-contained report might become two- or three-paragraph discussions in the summary report. Whereas the self-contained appraisal report assumes the full extent of the appraisal process should be apparent to the reader in the context of the report, the assumption is different with a summary appraisal report. As suggested by the ASB in an advisory opinion, "The reader of the Summary Appraisal Report should expect to find all significant data reported in tabular or abbreviated narrative formats."

Restricted Use Appraisal Report - The essential difference between the Self-Contained and Summary Appraisal Reports and the Restricted Use Appraisal Report is both the level of detail of presentation and a use restriction that limits the reliance on the report to the client and considers anyone else using the report an unintended user. The restricted use appraisal report is the only one of the three recognized appraisal reports that specifically limits the reliance of the report to the client and defines anyone else using the report an unintended user. Before entering into an agreement, the appraiser should establish with the client the situations where this type of report is to be used and should ensure that the client understands the restricted utility of the Restricted Use Report.

This standard also suggests that assumptions and limiting conditions established by the appraiser be grouped together in a section clearly identified in the appraisal report. Examples of assumptions and limiting conditions would include:

1.   The appraiser is not responsible for matters of a legal nature;

2.   Any sketch(es) in the report are approximate dimensions; and

3.   The appraiser is not required to give court testimony unless prior arrangements have been made.

In this day and time, it is very common, and in fact almost universal, for the appraiser to have a somewhat "boilerplate" section in the appraisal report for assumptions and limiting conditions. In fact, some appraisers will have a list containing as many as 40 or 50 assumptions or limiting conditions. Regardless of the extent to which the appraiser tries to limit his or her liability based on assumptions and limiting conditions, the Competency Rule still requires the appraiser to have the knowledge and experience necessary to properly undertake the appraisal assignment. By simply including a laundry list of assumptions and limiting conditions in his or her report, the appraiser has not circumvented the requirements of minimum competency.

Standards Rule 2-3 (Binding Requirement)

> **Each written real property appraisal report must contain a signed certification that is similar in content to the following form:**
>
> **I certify that, to the best of my knowledge and belief:**
>
> -- **the statements of fact contained in this report are true and correct.**
> -- **the reported analyses, opinions, and conclusions are limited only by the reported assumptions and limiting conditions, and are my personal, impartial and unbiased professional analyses, opinions, and conclusions.**
> -- **I have no (or the specified) present or prospective interest in the property that is the subject of this report, and no (or the specified) personal interest with respect to the parties involved.**
> -- **I have no bias with respect to the property that is the subject of this report or to the parties involved with this assignment .**
> -- **my engagement in this assignment was not contingent upon developing or reporting predetermined results.**
> -- **my compensation for completing this assignment is not contingent upon the development or reporting of a predetermined value or direction in value that favors the cause of the client, the amount of the value opinion, the attainment of a stipulated result, or the occurrence of a subsequent event directly related to the intended use of this appraisal.**
> -- **my analyses, opinions, and conclusions were developed, and this report has been prepared, in conformity with the Uniform Standards of Professional Appraisal Practice.**
> -- **I have (or have not) made a personal inspection of the property that is the subject of this report. (If more than one person signs the report, this certification must clearly specify which individuals did and which individuals did not make a personal inspection of the appraised property.)**
> -- **no one provided significant real property appraisal assistance to the person signing this certification. (If there are exceptions, the name of each individual providing significant real property appraisal assistance must be stated.)**

Standards Rule 2-3 is a binding requirement and is the certification statement of the appraiser. While the suggested certification statement appearing in Standards Rule 2-3 is just a model or suggested statement to be used, this particular statement has become widely accepted and today is used by many appraisers as the certification statement attached as an addendum to the report. S.R. 2-3 requires all appraisal reports, whether self-contained, summary, or restricted use, to contain a certification statement. In addition, an appraiser who signs any part of the appraisal report, including a letter of transmittal, must also sign this certification.

In the USPAP certification statement contained in Standards Rule 2-3, the appraiser must disclose any presence of prospective interest in the subject property as well as any personal interest or bias with respect to the parties involved. Present interest, for example, would extend to a real estate broker who has a current listing on the property and is asked to appraise the property for the purpose of financing the purchase price. Likewise, an appraiser could not appraise property in which he or she has a legal interest without disclosure. For example, an office building is owned by a partnership. One of the partners is a real estate appraiser. This person could not objectively appraise the office building. An example of personal interest or bias with respect to the parties involved would be if the subject property is owned by a relative of the appraiser. If a personal interest or potential bias does exist, Standards Rule 2-3 as well as the Ethics Rule requires *full disclosure* by the appraiser.

Standards Rule 2-3 does *not* recognize the acceptance of a contingency fee by the real property appraiser whenever he or she develops an opinion of value. In addition to Standards Rule 2-3, contingency fees for appraisers also are prohibited by the Management Section of the Ethics Rule.

In the vast majority of appraisal assignments, the appraiser, as well as perhaps others assisting the appraiser, will personally inspect the property. Regardless of whether the property is personally inspected, however, the certification statement must clearly indicate inspection or lack of inspection by the appraiser signing the certification.

If someone provides significant real property appraisal assistance to the appraiser who signs the certification, his or her name must be stated in the certification. The operative words of this certification statement are *significant real property appraisal assistance*. Examples of such assistance would include engineers, architects, and building inspectors. Significant appraisal assistance also would extend to the person who provided the cash flow/spreadsheet analysis on the subject property. This certification would not extend to persons merely providing clerical help in the preparation of the report. Any appraiser(s) who signs any part of the appraisal report must also sign the certification.

Standards Rule 2-4 (Specific Requirement)

An oral real property appraisal report must, at a minimum, address the substantive matters set forth in Standards Rule 2-2(b).

This standards rule, as noted, addresses the contents of an oral appraisal report. Standards Rule 2-4 is a specific requirement rather than a binding requirement. If the results of the appraisal assignment is an oral report, the appraiser must be sure that he or she follows the binding requirements of Standard 2(b), summary appraisal report, otherwise there is a violation of the uniform standards. Note the reference to S.R.2-2(a) and (b), which covers the reporting requirements for self-contained and summary appraisal reports.

Standard 2—Key Points

▸ Standard 2 governs the content and level of information required in an appraisal report.

▸ The standard covers communications to the client as well as to intended users.

▸ Standard 2 identifies three types of written appraisal reports: self-contained, summary, and restricted use.

▸ As a result of the two types of appraisals (complete and limited) recognized by Standard 1 and the three appraisal reports (self-contained, summary, restricted use) recognized by Standard 2, there are now six combinations of appraisals and appraisal reports:

▸ Three of the four standards rules are binding requirements.

▸ The appraiser must take extreme care to make certain the report will not be misleading.

▸ Both written and oral reports must present the analyses, opinions, and conclusions clearly and accurately.

▸ Minimum requirements must be included in all appraisal reports.

▸ Standard 2 suggests that assumptions and limiting conditions be grouped together in an identified section of the report.

▸ If information believed by the appraiser to be important is not available, the appraiser should explain the efforts undertaken to obtain the information.

▸ Each written real property appraisal report must contain a signed certification statement.

▸ Among other statements, the appraiser must certify that the appraisal report has been prepared in conformity with the USPAP.

▸ To the extent possible, an oral appraisal report must address the substantive matters of Standards Rule 2-2(b).

▸ If an appraiser signs any part of the appraisal report, including a letter of transmittal, he or she must also sign its certification.

Review Questions

1. Standard 2 suggests that assumptions and limiting conditions must be grouped together in an identified section of the appraisal report. Which of the following statements is an example of an assumption or limiting condition?

    A. I have (or have not) made a personal inspection of the property.

    B. The appraiser is not required to give testimony in court unless arrangements have been previously made.

    C. My compensation for preparing this report is $ _____.

    D. The appraiser has no (or the specified) present or prospective interest in the property that is the subject of this report.

2. In the certification statement as per Standards Rule 2-3, the appraiser should include which of the following statements?

    A. "The appraiser is not required to give testimony in court unless arrangements have been previously made."

    B. "I have no (or the specified) present or prospective interest in the property. . . ."

    C. "My compensation is contingent upon the reporting of a predetermined value. . . ."

    D. "My actual compensation for this assignment is $ _____."

3. Which of the following statements is correct in regard to an appraiser who signs any part of the appraisal report including a letter of transmittal?

    A. The appraiser must physically inspect the property before signing the report.

    B. If two appraisers sign the certification, each must receive fifty percent of the compensation.

    C. The appraiser must also sign the certification.

    D. If two appraisers are involved, each must contribute at least one-half of the time spent on preparing the report.

4. Which of the following statements is correct in regard to Standard 2 as it relates to self-contained appraisal reports?

    A. Communication must be in a manner that is not misleading.

    B. Recognized techniques must be used in the development of the appraisal.

    C. Proper communication extends to all readers of the report.

    D. Form but not content is addressed in this standard.

5. Standards Rule 2-3 addresses the certification statement in a written appraisal report. Which of the following statements is correct in regard to Standards Rule 2-3?

    A. Departure from this specific requirement is always permitted.
    B. The certification statement must be in a clearly marked separate section of the report.
    C. Each written appraisal report must contain a signed certification statement.
    D. The certification statement should identify whether or not the sketches in the appraisal report are drawn to scale.

6. In regard to the provisions and requirements of Standard 2, which of the following statements is correct?

    A. All of the standards rules of Standard 2 are binding requirements.
    B. Standard 2 only addresses written appraisal reports.
    C. The content and level of information required in a report are the subject of Standard 2.
    D. Standard 2 makes a certification statement optional by the appraiser.

7. Which of the following statements should be included in the certification required by Standard 2?

    A. "I have made a personal inspection of the property that is the subject of this report."
    B. "I have no present or prospective interest in the property that is the subject of this report."
    C. "My compensation is (or is not) contingent upon the reporting of a predetermined value or direction in value that favors the cause of the client."
    D. "The statements of fact contained in this report are true and correct."

8. Standards Rule 2-2(a) requires that each self-contained real property appraisal report contain certain minimum requirements. Which of the following items is required to be included in the report?

    A. The names of all possible readers of the report.
    B. The definition of market value as per the USPAP Glossary.
    C. The real property interest appraised.
    D. The date of the last sale of the property.

9. The certification statement required as per Standard 2 includes mention of persons involved in the appraisal assignment other than the person signing the certification. In regard to those persons, which of the following statements is correct?

   A. There should be a statement as to how much anyone providing significant real property appraisal assistance was compensated.
   B. The amount of time spent by each person providing the assistance must be stated.
   C. The name of each person providing significant real property appraisal assistance must be stated.
   D. The names of persons providing clerical assistance must be included.

10. Standard 2 requires the written appraisal report to include the effective date of the appraisal. Which of the following statements is correct as per the effective date?

    A. The effective date establishes the context of the value opinion.
    B. The effective date and the date of the report always will be the same date.
    C. The effective date cannot be a date later than the date of the report.
    D. The effective date should not be a date prior to the date of the report.

11. An appraiser should group the assumptions and limiting conditions in an identified section of the appraisal report. Which of the following statements is an example of an assumption or limiting condition?

    A. "I have made a personal inspection of the subject property."
    B. "This report is prepared in compliance with the USPAP."
    C. "No one offered significant appraisal assistance to the person preparing the report."
    D. "I assume that there are no hidden or unapparent conditions of the property that would render it more or less valuable."

12. The "operative" words in Standard 2 that result in the actions of an appraiser being referred to as an appraisal are

    A. collection of data.
    B. confirmation and reporting of data.
    C. analysis, opinion, and conclusion.
    D. application of the approaches to value.

13.	Standards Rule 2-4 addresses oral real property appraisal reports. In terms of this Standards Rule, which of the following statements is correct?

A.	Standards Rule 2-4 is directed toward the state regulatory agency that reviews experience requirements for appraisers through personal interviews with the appraiser.

B.	Standards Rule 2-4 addresses the responsibilities of a judge overseeing an eminent domain case as is further explained in Standard 3.

C.	Since this standards rule deal with oral real property appraisal reports, the Ethics Rule does not apply.

D.	At a minimum, the oral report must address the substantive matters as set forth in Standards Rule 2-2(b).

14.	Standard 2 identifies three types of written appraisal reports. Which of the following appraisal reports is recognized in Standard 2?

A.	Self-contained
B.	Restricted User
C.	Limited Departure
D.	Summarized

15.	Which of the following combinations of appraisals and appraisal reports is recognized by the USPAP?

A.	Restricted Use/Self-contained
B.	Limited/Summarized
C.	Complete/Restricted Use
D.	Complete/Limited

Standard 3

REAL PROPERTY AND PERSONAL PROPERTY APPRAISAL REVIEW, DEVELOPMENT AND REPORTING

Standard 3 states:

In performing an appraisal review assignment involving a real property or personal property appraisal, an appraiser acting as a reviewer must develop and report a credible opinion as to the quality of another appraiser's work and must clearly disclose the scope of work performed in the assignment.

Standard 3 is directed toward the activities associated with developing and communicating an opinion in regard to the quality of work performed by someone else in either a real property or personal property appraisal assignment. This standard must be understood by anyone who finds himself or herself in the role of reviewing someone else's appraisals. While the specifics of establishing and maintaining an effective review appraisal procedure are not the subject matter to be addressed in this text, a general overview of the functions of a review appraiser operating within the specifics of Standard 3 reveal some interesting points.

First, the process of reviewing the work performed by someone else goes far beyond checking someone's appraisal for completeness to see if the appraiser has "crossed the t's and dotted the i's." Reviewing, as used within the context of Standard 3, requires the preparation of a separate report or file memorandum. More specifically, what sets review appraisal apart from simply checking for completeness is that the review appraiser makes comments, renders opinions, and reaches conclusions.

Second, because the review appraiser is rendering opinions concerning the work or service performed by the appraiser, the Competency Rule of the USPAP applies to the review appraiser just as it applies to the fee appraiser who prepared the report being reviewed. Therefore, prior to reviewing an appraisal prepared by someone else, the review appraiser must have the *knowledge* and *experience* necessary to develop credible appraisal review opinions. Otherwise, he or she is in violation of the Competency Rule.

Third, if the review appraiser undertakes to "redo" the appraisal to fit his or her conclusions, then the review appraiser may find that he or she now is governed by either Standard 1 or Standard 2. If such is the case, then the review appraiser would have to be in compliance with Standards 1 and 2.

Finally, if the appraisal review report is misleading or fraudulent, the review appraiser is in violation of the Ethics Rule. All four sections of the Ethics Rule extend to review appraisal work.

Standard 3 is a free standing standard. Unlike the appraisal of real property (Standards 1 and 2) or personal property(Standards 4 and 5), the process of review appraisal assignments and the reporting of those results are both contained in a single standard.

Standards Rule 3-1   (Binding Requirement)

In developing an appraisal review, the reviewer must:

(a)   **identify the reviewer's client and intended users, the intended use of the reviewer's opinions and conclusions and the purpose of the review assignment;**

(b)   **identify the:**
  (i)   **subject of the appraisal review assignment,**
  (ii)   **date of the review;**
  (iii)   **property and ownership interest appraised (if any) in the work under review,**
  (iv)   **date of the work under review and the effective date of the opinion in the work under review, and**
  (v)   **appraiser(s) who completed the work under review, unless the identify was withheld;**

(c)   **identify the scope of work to be performed;**

(d)   **develop an opinion as to the completeness of the material under review within the scope of work applicable in the assignment;**

(e)   **develop an opinion as to the apparent adequacy and relevance of the data and the propriety of any adjustments to the data;**

(f)   **develop an opinion as to the appropriateness of the appraisal methods and techniques used and develop the reasons for any disagreement;**

(g) develop an opinion as to whether the analyses, opinions, and conclusions in the work under review are appropriate and reasonable, and develop the reasons for any disagreement.

Standards Rule 3-1, which is a binding requirement, establishes the proper framework to be followed in the review process. To comply with the provisions of Standards Rule 3-1, the review appraiser must have the expertise and experience necessary to correctly form an opinion about the accuracy and completeness of the appraisal report being reviewed. Standard 3 does provide for a difference in the review appraiser's opinion of value from that rendered in the appraisal report, provided:

1. the reviewer's scope of work in developing his or her value opinion must not be less than the scope of work applicable to the original appraisal assignment;

2. the reviewer may use additional information available to him or her that was not available to the original appraiser in the development of his or her value opinion.

Standards Rule 3-2   (Binding Requirement)

In reporting the results of an appraisal review, the reviewer must communicate each analysis, opinion, and conclusion in a manner that is not misleading.

In reporting the results of an appraisal review, the reviewer appraiser must:

(a) **state the identity of the client, by name or type, and intended users; the intended use of the assignment results; and the purpose of the assignment;**

(b) **state the information that must be identified in accordance with Standards Rule 3-1(b);**

(c) **state the nature, extent, and detail of the review process undertaken (i.e., the scope of work identified in accordance with Standards Rule 3-1(c);**

(d) **state the opinions, reasons, and conclusions required in Standards Rule 3-1 (d-g), given the scope of work identified in compliance with Standards Rule 3-1(c);**

(e) **include all known pertinent information; and**

(f) **include a signed certification similar in content to the following:**

I certify that, to the best of my knowledge and belief:

-- **the facts and data reported by the review appraiser and used in the review process are true and correct.**

-- **the analyses, opinions, and conclusions in this review report are limited only by the assumptions and limiting conditions stated in this review report, and are my personal, impartial and unbiased professional analyses, opinions, and conclusions.**

-- **I have no (or the specified) present or prospective interest in the property that is the subject of this report, and no (or the specified) personal interest with respect to the parties involved.**

-- **I have no bias with respect to the property that is the subject of this report or to the parties involved with this assignment.**

-- **my engagement in this assignment was not contingent upon developing or reporting predetermined results.**

-- **my compensation is not contingent on an action or event resulting from the analyses, opinions, or conclusions in, or the use of this review report.**

-- **my analyses, opinions, and conclusions were developed and this review report was prepared in conformity with the Uniform Standards of Professional Appraisal Practice.**

-- **I did not (did) personally inspect the subject property of the report under review.**

-- **no one provided significant real or personal property appraisal or appraisal review assistance to the person signing this certification. (If there are exceptions, the name of each individual(s) providing real or personal appraisal or appraisal review assistance must be stated.)**

Standards Rule 3-2 is to the review appraiser as Standard 2 is to the appraiser—namely, it covers communications. As is true with Standards Rule 3-1, Standards Rule 3-2 is also a binding requirement. In addition, just as Standard 2 contains the requirement of a certification statement as part of the appraisal report, Standard 3 contains a certification statement by the review appraiser. Included in the certification must be a statement that the review report was prepared "in conformity with the Uniform Standards of Professional Appraisal Practice."

Standards Rule 3-3   (Binding Requirement)

An oral appraisal review report must address the substantive matters set forth in Standards Rule 3-2.

Standards Rule 3-2 addresses the subject matter of oral appraisal reviews. Simply stated, this standards rule requires the reviewer giving an oral review to follow the procedure outlined and explained in Standards Rule 3-2.

Standard 3—Key Points

▸ Standard 3 governs appraisal review.

▸ The standard covers both the actual review process and reporting the results of that review and all of Standard 3 is a binding requirement.

▸ Reviewing as envisioned in Standard 3 goes beyond checking someone's appraisal for completeness.

▸ The Competency Rule applies to the reviewer just as it applies to the person who prepared the report being reviewed.

▸ A review appraiser must have the knowledge and experience necessary to complete the review competently.

▸ As a result of rendering a difference of opinion, analysis, or conclusion, the review appraiser may find that he or she is governed by Standard 1 or Standard 2.

▸ If the appraisal review is misleading or fraudulent, the review appraiser may be in violation of the Ethics Rule.

▸ Standard 3 requires a signed certification statement by the reviewer.

Review Questions

1. Which of the following statements is correct in regard to Standard 3?

    A. Any comments or opinions of the reviewer should be made directly on the original appraisal report.
    B. A reviewer must take appropriate steps to identify the precise extent of the review process to be completed in an assignment.
    C. A review appraiser must not form an opinion regarding the adequacy and appropriateness of the report being reviewed.
    D. The review process consists entirely of checking for completeness and consistency in the report.

2. In reviewing an appraisal report, a reviewer develops his or her own opinion of value. If the reviewer wishes to express that opinion, he or she must take which of the following steps?

   A. The reviewer's scope of work in developing his or her value opinion must not be less than the scope of work applicable to the original appraisal assignment.
   B. Physically inspect the subject property.
   C. Identify and set forth any additional properties ever appraised by the reviewer.
   D. Clearly identify and disclose all assumptions and limitations connected with the different estimate of value.

3. A review appraiser is required to include a signed certification statement when reporting the results of an appraisal review. Which of the following statements should be part of the certification statement?

   A. "I have not give court testimony in regard to this appraisal report."
   B. "I did not (did) personally inspect the subject property of the report under review."
   C. "My compensation is (is not) contingent on an action or event resulting from the analyses, opinions and conclusions in, or the use of, this review report."
   D. "This review report was prepared in conformity with Standard 9 of the Uniform Standards of Professional Appraisal Practice."

4. In regard to the review process, which of the following statements is corrct?

   A. A misleading or fraudulent appraisal review report does not violate the Ethics Rule.
   B. The Competency Rule does not apply to the reviewer.
   C. The review appraiser must clearly disclose the nature of the review process undertaken.
   D. Review appraisers simply check for a level of completeness by the appraiser.

5. In reviewing an appraisal, an appraiser must

   A. identify any property that he or she has previously appraised.
   B. use all three of the appraisal methods.
   C. not use additional information available to him or her that was not available to the original appraiser.
   D. develop an opinion as to the completeness of the material under review within the scope of work applicable in the assignment.

6.   Which of the following statements best explains the most obvious difference between the real property appraisal standard(s) and the real or personal property review standard?

   A.   Both the real property appraisal standards and the review standard have binding requirements.
   B.   Whereas the appraisal of real property involves two distinct standards, the review process is covered under a single standard.
   C.   The Ethics Rule does not apply to the review standard.
   D.   Both the appraiser conducting the appraisal and the reviewer must comply with the Competency Rule.

7.   For the person who is functioning as a review appraiser, which of the following statements is correct?

   A.   A misleading review does not violate the Ethics Rule.
   B.   The Competency Rule does not apply to the reviewer and the review process.
   C.   The nature of the review process undertaken should be clearly disclosed.
   D.   If the appraisal is a form report, the review appraiser should sign the appraisal report under review at the bottom of the back page.

8.   In regard to the signed certification statement by a review appraiser, which of the following statements is correct?

   A.   Inclusion of the certification statement is a specific requirement.
   B.   If anyone provides the review appraiser with significant real or personal property appraisal or appraisal review assistance, his or her name may be omitted.
   C.   The reviewer is not permitted to inspect the subject property.
   D.   The certification statement should certify that the facts and data reported and used are true and correct.

Standards 4-10

The remaining seven standards included in the USPAP cover topics not directly addressed in this manual. The specific areas covered in the remaining standards are:

Standard 4   Real Estate/Real Property Consulting, Development

Standard 5   Real Estate/Real Property Consulting, Reporting

Standard 6   Mass Appraisal, Development and Reporting

Standard 7   Personal Property Appraisal, Development

Standard 8   Personal Property Appraisal, Reporting

Standard 9   Business Appraisal, Development

Standard 10   Business Appraisal, Reporting

Standard 4—Real Property Appraisal Consulting, Development

Standard 4 states:

In developing real property appraisal consulting assignments, an appraiser must identify the problem to be solved and the scope of work necessary to solve the problem, and correctly complete research and analysis necessary to produce credible results.

The wording of Standard 4 is similar to the wording of Standard 1 but is directed toward the performance of a real property consulting assignment undertaken by an appraiser to develop, without advocacy, an analysis, recommendation or opinion where at least one opinion of value is a component of the analysis leading to the assignment results. Standard 4 recognizes that the phrase "appraisal consulting" involves an opinion of value but does not have an appraisal or an appraisal review as its primary purpose.

All of the Preamble and Rules of the USPAP applies to Standard 4. Persons engaged in appraisal consulting services should pay close attention to the Management Section of the Ethics Rule and the Competency Rule. In addition, if an opinion of value is used as part of an appraisal consulting assignment, the opinion must be developed within the context of Standard 1.

Standard 5—Real Property Appraisal Consulting, Reporting

Standard 5 states:

In reporting the results of a real property appraisal consulting assignment, an appraiser must communicate each analysis, opinion, and conclusion in a manner that is not misleading.

Standard 5, the consulting reporting standard, is to Standard 4 what Standard 2 is to Standard 1. Accordingly, the standard is specific and in some cases binding in terms of what should and must be reported in the analysis, opinion and conclusion stated in the real property appraisal consulting assignment.

As is true with Standard 2, an appraiser communicating a written consulting assignment must include a signed certification statement in the appraisal consulting report. The certification statement for a real property appraisal consulting assignment is very similar to that required in a real property appraisal assignment. As is true with real property appraisal assignments, the appraiser developing and communicating a real property consulting assignment must state all of the extraordinary assumptions and hypothetical conditions under which the appraisal consulting assignment was completed.

Standard 6—Mass Appraisal, Development and Reporting

Standard 6 states:

In developing a mass appraisal, an appraiser must be aware of, understand, and correctly employ those generally accepted methods and techniques necessary to produce and communicate credible appraisals.

Standard 6 addresses the activities associated with developing and communicating the appraisal of a universe of properties. Such activities are normally undertaken for purposes of ad valorem taxation. The USPAP defines mass appraisal as "the process of valuing a universe of properties as of a given date utilizing standard methodology, employing common data, and allowing for statistical testing."

The vast majority of real estate appraisers do not undertake mass appraisal assignments for purposes of ad valorem taxation. Those appraisers who do, however, should pay close attention to the Jurisdictional Exception Rule that may apply to several sections of Standard 6 because of the variations in municipal, county and state laws.

Standard 7—Personal Property Appraisal, Development

Standard 7 states:

In developing a personal property appraisal, an appraiser must identify the problem to be solved and the scope of work necessary to solve the problem, and correctly complete research and analysis necessary to produce a credible appraisal.

Standard 7 is directed toward the same substantive aspects addressed in Standard 1, but it covers the appraisal of personal property. The USPAP defines personal property as "identifiable portable and tangible objects which are considered by the general public as being personal, e.g. furnishings, artwork, antiques, gems and jewelry, collectibles, machinery and equipment; all tangible property that is not classified as real estate."

The appraisal of personal property requires knowledge and experience different from that required to appraise real property. As noted in Standards Rule 1-2 (e), an appraiser must "identify the characteristics of the property that are relevant to the purpose and intended use of the appraisal, including any personal property, trade fixtures, or intangible items that are not real property but are included in the appraisal." Therefore, additional expertise in personal property appraisal may be required and, if so, the personal property appraisal is bound by Standards 7 and 8.

Standard 8—Personal Property Appraisal Reporting

Standard 8 states:

In reporting the results of a personal property appraisal, an appraiser must communicate each analysis, opinion, and conclusion in a manner that is not misleading.

In regard to appraisal reporting requirements, Standard 8 is identical in scope and purpose to the contents of Standard 2. The standard contains guidelines similar in wording to that contained in Standard 2 and Standard 5. The reporting of a personal property appraisal requires a certification statement similar to the one suggested in Standard 2.

Standard 9—Business Appraisal, Development

Standard 9 states:

In developing a business or intangible asset appraisal, an appraiser must identify the problem to be solved and the scope of work necessary to solve the problem, and correctly complete the research and analysis steps necessary to produce a credible appraisal.

Standard 9 is directed toward the same substantive aspects addressed in Standard 1, but covers business and intangible asset appraisal. As is true with all ten standards, the Preamble and Rules, including the Ethics Rule and the Competency Rule, extends to business and intangible asset appraisals.

Standard 10—Business Appraisal, Reporting

Standard 10 states:

In reporting the results of a business or intangible asset appraisal an appraiser must communicate each analysis, opinion, and conclusion in a manner that is not misleading.

In regard to appraisal reporting requirements, Standard 10 is similar in scope and purpose to the contents of Standard 2. As is true with all of the applicable reporting standards, a written business appraisal must contain a signed certification statement. The certification statement is similar in content to the certification contained in Standard 2.

A current copy of Standards 4 through 10 can be obtained from the Appraisal Foundation's subscription service.

Statements

Statements on Appraisal Standards are authorized by the bylaws of the Appraisal Foundation. The statements are issued to clarify, interpret, explain, and elaborate the USPAP and are intended to assist the appraiser, client, user and the general public in understanding the standards. Statements have the same weight as the Standards Rules and can only be adopted by the ASB after exposure and adequate time for comments.

As of January 1, 2002, the ASB has issued ten Statements on Appraisal Standards. The effective dates on these statements are published in the USPAP and copies of the Statements on Appraisal Standards can be obtained from the Appraisal Foundation. Three of the statements have been retired.

INDEX TO STATEMENTS

SMT-1   Appraisal Review --- Clarification of Comment on Standards Rule 3-1(g). Adopted July 8, 1991; Retired September 15, 1999.

The subject matter of this statement was incorporated into Standard 3, effective January 1, 2000. Thus the standard was retired. The numbering and place of this statement was retained for editorial consistency.

SMT-2   Discounted Cash Flow Analysis. Adopted July 8, 1991; Revised September 16, 1998.

The issue addressed in SMT-2 concerns the use and acceptance of discounted cash flow analysis. Discounted cash flow (DCF) is recognized as a generally accepted method for evaluating the feasibility of an investment. The person using DCF as part of the analysis is fully responsible for the assumptions of DCF as well as the resulting output; thus, the results should be tested and checked for errors and reasonableness. The basis for this responsibility lies within Standards Rules 1-1 (b) and (c), which address the commitment of errors of omission and commission that significantly affect the appraisal. In addition, when using discounted cash flow analysis, the appraiser should cite the name and version of the software he or she is using and provide a brief description of the methods and assumptions inherent in the software.

SMT-3   Retrospective Value Opinions. Adopted July 8, 1991; Revised September 16, 1998.

Standards Rule 2-2 (a)(b)(c)(vi) and Standards Rule 8-2(a)(b)(c)(vi) require that an appraisal report contain the effective date of the appraisal and the date of the report. Retrospective appraisals, where the effective date of the appraisal report is prior to the date of the report, may be necessary for property tax matters, condemnation proceedings, and similar situations. For retrospective value estimates, the appraiser is advised to use wording such as "the retrospective market value was" rather than "the market value is." Careful wording will help eliminate confusion by the reader of the appraisal report.

For a retrospective value estimate, the appraisal is complicated by the fact that the appraiser knows what has occurred in the marketplace since the effective date of the appraisal. When choosing market data to be analyzed, the appraiser should pick an appropriate cutoff date because beyond some point the subsequent date will not reflect the relevant market.

SMT-4   Prospective Value Opinions. Adopted July 8, 1991; Revised September 15, 1999.

This statement covers the substantive aspects of a prospective value estimate. As required in Standards Rule 2-2 (a)(b)(c)(vi) and Standards Rule 8-2(a)(b)(c)(vi), the appraisal must specify the effective date as well as the date of the report. Prospective appraisals, where the effective date of the appraisal is subsequent to the date of the report, may, for example, occur in the appraisal of a proposed development For prospective value estimates, the appraiser is advised to use wording such as "the prospective market value is expected to be" and not "the market value is." Careful wording will assist the reader in understanding the appraisal.

Prospective value estimates should be based on the market support of the forecasts when made. In addition, evidence that the proposed improvements can be completed by the stated effective date is important. All value estimates should be made with clear reference to the time frame within which the analysis was made to establish a point of reference concerning the market conditions and assumptions.

SMT-5   Confidentiality Section of the Ethics Rule. Adopted September 10, 1991; Revised September 15, 1999; Retired July 1, 2001.

The Ethics Rule of the USPAP contains four sections, one of which is confidentiality. An appraiser must protect the confidential nature of the appraiser-client relationship; however, the obligation of the appraiser to protect this confidentiality is neither absolute nor clearly understood.

As stated in this statement, the confidential matters of an appraisal are the appraiser's assignment results, which as defined in the USPAP are "an appraiser's opinions and conclusions developed specific to an assignment." Such information can be disclosed only to the three groups cited in the confidentiality section of the Ethics Rule. Factual information obtained from a client that is not deemed confidential, however, may be disclosed by the appraiser without the client's permission. To hold that any and all information obtained from the client is confidential just because it came from the client is an extremely broad interpretation that burdens the appraiser and diminishes the quality of appraisal services.

The client is in the best position to know what information should be treated as confidential. Information given by the client to other parties, such as a potential buyer or lender, does not become confidential just because it is given to the appraiser. All other information obtained by the appraiser should not be deemed confidential unless the appraiser knows of the confidential nature of the data.

Recently it has been noted that parts of Statement 5 conflict with aspects of the Gramm-Leach-Bliley Act as well as the Federal Trade Commission's Final Rule on Privacy of Consumer Financial Information. Therefore, the ASB has retired this statement until it can be rewritten to more accurately reflect the issue of privacy laws and regulations.

SMT-6   Reasonable Exposure Time in Real Property and Personal Property Market Value Opinions. Adopted September 16,1993; Revised September 15, 1999.

The USPAP makes reference to the need for the appraiser to be specific in estimating the exposure time associated with the opinion of value. Thus, the question becomes, how is this reasonable time estimated? The further question is, when is it presumed to occur? Does it occur prior to or after the effective date of the appraisal? Exposure time is always presumed to precede the effective date of the appraisal.

Exposure time is defined as the "estimated length of time the property interest being appraised would have been offered on the market prior to the hypothetical consummation of a sale at market value on the effective date of the appraisal." Clearly, the exposure time will vary from property type to property type and under various market conditions. The estimate of exposure time can be expressed as a range and can be based on such things as statistical information regarding days on the market, information gathered through sales verification, and interviews of market participants. The ASB also suggests that the discussion of exposure time appear in an appropriate section of the appraisal report and that it be referenced at the statement of the value definition and value conclusion. Further, the appraiser should estimate exposure time within the context of the type of real estate being appraised and the value range being estimated, rather than as an isolated time period.

SMT-7   Permitted Departure from Specific Requirements in Real Property and Personal Property Appraisal Assignments. Adopted March 22, 1994; Revised September 15, 1999.

This statement is the direct result of the ASB attempting to address the confusion surrounding the appropriate time to invoke the Departure Rule in performing real property appraisals, and the necessary reporting requirements when the Rule is utilized. The uncertainty has resulted in many appraisers being afraid to accept a limited appraisal assignment for fear they would be in violation of the USPAP. If the appraiser can determine that the request by a knowledgeable client for something less than a complete appraisal would not result in a misleading analysis and report, then the appraiser can invoke the Departure Rule and the assignment can be accepted and performed. However, in order to accept a limited appraisal assignment, the appraiser must know the client's understanding of the type of real estate, the market conditions involved and the intended use of the appraisal.

Both complete and limited appraisals are now defined in the USPAP. In addition, Standards Rules 2-2 and 8-2, both binding requirements, set forth three options for any written appraisal report: (1) self-contained, (2) summary and (3) restricted use. The reliability of the results of either a complete or limited appraisal developed under Standard 1 or Standard 7 is not affected by the type of report prepared under Standard 2 or Standard 8.

SMT-8   Electronic Transmission of Reports. Adopted July 18, 1995; Revised September 16, 1998; Retired July 1, 2001.

When this statement was originally adopted, the ASB concluded that an electronically transmitted report is indeed a written report and thus must meet the minimum USPAP reporting requirements including a signed certification. Appraisers were expected to take the necessary steps to protect the data integrity of such reports. The software used to transfer it was to provide, as a minimum, a digital signature security feature for all appraisers signing a report. A report carrying such a signature carried the same authenticity as an ink signature on a copy report. The Record Keeping Section of the Ethics Rule applies to all such reports.

Unfortunately, this statement, originally adopted in 1995, did not envision the technological changes that have occurred in recent years in terms of transporting appraisals over the Internet. As a result of these technological changes, the contents of this statement have become obsolete. The ASB plans to readdress the subject matter of SMT-8.

SMT-9   Identification of the Client's Intended Use in Developing and Reporting Appraisal, Appraisal Review, or Consulting Assignment Opinions and Conclusions. Adopted August 27, 1996; Revised September 15, 1999.

This statement concerns the importance of carefully identifying the client and other parties who will use the report (without violating the Confidentiality Section of the Ethics Rule), along with identifying the "intended use" of the appraisal. This information must be stated in the report itself. If the client's identity is omitted from the report, it must be made a part of the appraiser's workfile. All identifications, as well as the obligations the appraiser has to the client and intended users, must be established with the client prior to the appraiser's acceptance of the assignment. SMT-9 also offers illustrations of appropriate wording that could be used to properly make the required identifications.

SMT-10   Assignments for Use by a Federally Insured Depository Institution in a Federally Related Transaction. Adopted July 1, 2000.

The issues addressed in this statement are a direct result of the federal financial institution regulatory agencies conclusion that some appraisers have not followed USPAP as well as the regulations of the regulatory agencies. This lack of compliance is especially true in appraisals of commercial real estate and residential tract development projects. The regulatory agencies' concerns cover three specific appraisal areas: USPAP compliance, appraiser independence, and appraisal review.

Appraisers should fully understand what USPAP requires of the appraiser when a federally insured depository institution is involved. In addition, any appraiser engaged by a federally insured depository institution must know how that institution's regulations and guidelines affect the appraiser's scope of work and the report content requirements.

Statement 10's requirements are applicable and binding when the purpose of the appraisal assignment includes developing an opinion of market value that will be used by an institution in a federally related transaction. Any appraiser engaged to perform appraisal assignments for a federally insured depository institution should, in addition to knowing this statement, have a copy of the applicable regulatory agency rules.

Case Studies

Case studies are included in this book to present situations in which provisions and sections of the USPAP may have been violated. The answers to some of the questions are quite clear and direct. Other cases, however, do not have "easy answers."

The cases are intended to make the reader think about the application of the uniform standards and to draw conclusions from the standards in light of the information presented. Suggestions concerning how each case may be analyzed appear in Appendix C. However, the answers suggested should not be considered to be "cast in concrete." The subjective nature of the case situations as well as the interpretation of certain provisions in the USPAP may cause different people to arrive at different solutions. What is important to realize is that as a result of the USPAP now being recognized and accepted as the uniform standards of the appraisal profession, both appraisers and the users of appraisal services now have a "playbook" by which actions can be measured. Some of the activities discussed in these cases may be the way things were once done but not the way they are to be done now.

Case 1

John develops motels throughout the region. He is interested in constructing a 100-unit motel in the town where Bob has his appraisal practice. John contacts Bob and discusses the proposed project with him, stressing the fact that $2,250,000 will need to be borrowed to "make the thing go." The developer tells Bob that he is not interested in spending a lot of money on an appraisal but if Bob can arrange for the financing, a "big" appraisal fee will be available. Bob tells the developer that he sees no reason why he can't come up with the $2,250,000 number and in fact goes on to say, "Go ahead and tell the lender you have an appraisal for more than what you need." Two days later, Bob receives a letter from the developer informing him that his appraisal services will be needed to "finalize" what was discussed. A $20,000 fee is quoted as compensation for the appraisal.

A. Has Bob made an appraisal?

B. Has Bob violated any of the sectionss of the USPAP? If yes, what has he violated?

C. If you answered "yes" to Question B, what should Bob have done when the developer explained what he was trying to do?

Case 2

Jane, a certified appraiser, is a resident in a subdivision that has seen property tax assessments increase an average of 50 percent during the past year. At a neighborhood meeting, the president of the neighborhood association, who knows Jane is an appraiser, suggests that the association employ Jane to reappraise all of the homes in the neighborhood and, in turn, represent the association before the local tax appeal board. Everyone agrees this is a good idea and a unanimous vote is taken, each owner agreeing to pay Jane $100. "Of course, Jane," the president said, "you'll have to pay yourself the $100 for your own house." Jane prepares separate appraisals for every home in the neighborhood and appears before the tax appeal board. Her argument is so convincing that the appeal board lowers every owner's assessed value back to the previous year's level. Everyone concludes the $100 per owner was money well spent.

    A.   Has Jane violated any section or rule of the USPAP? Explain.

    B.   Regardless of your answer in Question A, what should Jane have included in the certification statement accompanying each appraisal report?

Case 3

Ed has owned and operated a very successful regional appraisal firm for more than 20 years. He is state certified as a general appraiser, holds two prestigious "income property" designations, and teaches appraisal courses at the local community college.

Ed runs into an old college buddy, Bob, whom he has not seen in 25 years. During the conversation, Bob finds out that Ed is a real estate appraiser and remarks that he also "dabbles in real estate." If fact, he has his eyes on a vacant site down on Jefferson Street. "They want $3 per square foot for it and I just don't think it's worth more than $2 per square foot." Ed responds, "You know you're probably right. I just appraised two tracts on Jefferson, one of which sold for $2 per square foot and the other sold for $2.10 per square foot."

The next day, Ed receives a call from Bob who, after telling him how good it was to see an old friend, asks Ed if he would send him some information on that property they discussed because Ed says, "I really want to buy it." Bob goes on to tell Ed that he would be happy to pay him for his time.

Ed takes a map of the area and identifies the two parcels he had previously appraised and the property Bob had discussed with him. In the letter to Bob, Ed notes that the property was close to the other two sales and in fact was "probably about the same." Along with this information, Ed sends a bill for $200. Two days later, Bob calls to say "thanks for the information." Three days later, a check for $200 arrives. Ed never hears anything else from Bob.

The next conversation Ed has in regard to the property is when Bob's attorney calls six months later. He informs Ed that after Bob bought the property for "the $2 per square foot you told him to pay," leaking underground storage tanks were found on the property. The attorney told Bob that "everyone knows there once was a gasoline station on that property." The attorney goes on to tell Ed that, "We're suing you for that lousy appraisal you did." Ed's response is that he did not do an appraisal, rather "I was just helping out an old buddy."

A.   According to the USPAP, has Ed made an appraisal? Explain why or why not.

B.   If he has made an appraisal, which rules or standards rules has he violated?

C.   Would your answers to Question A and Question B have been the same had Ed not collected the $200 fee?

Case 4

A well-known regional real estate developer recently announced plans for rehabilitating a large vacant warehouse located in the central business district into retail commercial space. The tenants will be retail shops, restaurants, and bars. The city is in full support of the project and when the announcement was made, the mayor was at the press conference to announce that the city was "assisting with some of the financing" as well as providing certain improvements such as street improvements, sidewalks, etc.

The developer contacts Frank, a real estate appraiser, and informs him of the plans. No formal plans or specs are available, but that should not be a problem because the developer tells Frank that an insurance company is ready to provide "all the money we need." Frank is asked to appraise the property as if it were fully occupied and under the assumption of a below-market interest rate because the insurance company is going to have a small equity position once the project is up and running.

A.   Can Frank appraise the property without a set of plans and specifications?

B.   Can Frank appraise the property as if it were fully occupied?

C.   Does the below-market interest rate impact the appraised value?

D.   What standards rules cover plans and specs, full occupancy, and below-market financing?

E.   Should Frank accept this appraisal assignment under the conditions and constraints stated?

Case 5

Phillip appraises all types of real and personal property. Reluctantly, he became state certified as a general appraiser because he knew certification would increase his workload and probably his income. Because Phillip is not a member of one of the private appraisal organizations that wrote the uniform standards, he sees no reason to follow them. In his appraisal reports, he makes no reference to the USPAP and in fact does not even have a copy of the uniform standards. No one seems to complain about his work product and Phillip wonders if his clients really care whether he follows the uniform standards.

A. Do the uniform standards apply to Phillip?

B. If your answer to Question A is "yes," explain how they apply since he does not make mention of them in his appraisal reports.

C. Can Phillip be forced to reference the USPAP in his appraisal reports? Explain.

Case 6

Christine completed an appraisal assignment, the purpose of which was to estimate the market value for a vacant tract of land. She was in somewhat of a hurry when she was writing the report and forgot to put a section on highest and best use in her report. She did, however, discuss highest and best use, and, in fact, she placed a highest and best use section in her workfile.

A.   By not including a separate section on highest and best use in the appraisal report, has Christine violated any part of the USPAP? Explain.

B.   What should she do now that she has discovered her mistake?

Case 7

Because hard times were being felt throughout the area, a bank has had to foreclose on numerous loans. Jane, a residential appraiser, accepts an assignment to appraise a house located on ten acres of land. The purpose of the appraisal is to estimate the likely sales price at foreclosure for the bank. When Jane arrives at the entrance to the property, she is met by an angry owner who informs her that "no one will step foot on my property." The owner, along with his 12-gauge shotgun, makes a convincing argument. When Jane relays what happened back to the lender, she is told to go ahead and do the best job she can and not to worry about actually inspecting the property.

A. Does Jane have to inspect the property as part of the appraisal assignment?

B. If your answer to Question A is "no," then what steps should she take to fully comply with the USPAP?

C. What documentation should Jane include in her report to show the steps she has taken to complete the assignment as directed?

Case 8

As a result of major flooding in the area, many of the homes in Pete's city have received extensive water damage. A national appraisal firm has received the contract from an insurance company to appraise the 100 homes in the area insured by this particular insurance company. Pete is contacted by the appraisal firm to see if he would be interested in appraising the homes because he is certified in that state and familiar with the area. Pete is to receive 65 percent of what the appraisal firm receives and he will be paid directly by the firm. Pete agrees to take the assignment.

A.   Can Pete accept this type of compensation?

B.   Has Pete violated any sections of the USPAP?

Case 9

Ken is contacted by a client who informs Ken that a neighbor is "thinking about selling his house" and needs someone to tell him what it is worth. Ken is given the person's name. The next day, Ken calls the person, introduces himself, and agrees to appraise the house for $400. An appointment is made for the following morning. When Ken arrives at the house, he inspects the outside, takes a few pictures, and knocks on the front door. The man who opens the door introduces himself as Don, the person to whom Ken talked to yesterday. Don introduces the woman in the living room as his wife, Sarah. Ken completes the inspection, takes the necessary measurements, and leaves.

Two days later, Sarah telephones Ken to see if he has come up with a final figure. Ken says, "Yes, I feel that the house is worth $150,000." Sarah thanks Ken for his promptness and hangs up. An hour later, Ken receives another telephone call. This time the caller is Don who is not too happy. He informs Ken that "I employed you, and you had no right to tell her what the property was worth." Don goes on to tell Ken that Sarah is suing him for divorce and the house is part of the divorce settlement.

    A.   Who is Ken's client?

    B.   Should Ken have given the opinion of value to Sarah over the telephone? Why or why not?

    C.   What if Don had called? Should Ken have given him the opinion of value over the telephone? Why or why not?

    D.   Which standards rules, if any, may have been violated by Ken?

Case 10

Roger is the only state certified general appraiser in his town. While the town is not very large, it does contain a small shopping center and a 100-unit apartment complex. Because he now is state certified, Roger decides to advertise his business by having a multicolor brochure printed. On the brochure, he states, "all types of properties appraised." Because everyone in the town knows the mall and the 100-unit apartment complex, Roger includes a picture of both properties on the brochure to give it a "local flavor." Because Roger has never appraised either one of these properties, he doesn't mention them by name in the brochure.

A.   Is Roger in violation of any rules or standard of the USPAP?

B.   Assuming Roger had indeed appraised both of these properties, could he include a picture of them in his brochure without being in violation of the USPAP?

Case 11

Mike was employed to complete an appraisal assignment in 1998. The purpose of the appraisal assignment was to render an opinion concerning the market value of a farm that was part of a condemnation proceeding for the expansion of an airport. The date of the value estimate was January 10, 1998, and Mike completed the appraisal report on February 7, 1999. Mike testified in court on September 20, 2000. The opposition won the appeal and the attorney who had employed Mike appealed the case to the state supreme court. The state supreme court made its final ruling on July 30, 2001. Once the state supreme court made its final ruling, Mike destroyed all of his files from this assignment; however, he did keep a copy of the appraisal that he had given the attorney back in 1999.

     A.   Has Mike violated any part of the USPAP?

     B.   If your answer to Question A is "yes," what has he violated?

     C.   How long should Mike keep the information in his files?

Case 12

Larry has been a fee appraiser for City National Bank for more than ten years. Since 1987, he has used the USPAP as a guide for seeing that all his appraisals are in full compliance. In fact, he gave his lender a copy of the uniform standards when they were first published. Recently, his lender was told that the Office of the Comptroller of the Currency (OCC) had implemented some rules that required more in terms of "standards" than what is covered in the USPAP. When the lender mentioned this to Larry, the response from Larry was, "I follow the USPAP and that is all I have to do. The other stuff does not apply to me."

A. Does that "other stuff" apply to Larry? Explain.

B. Is Larry in violation of the USPAP if he does not incorporate regulatory agency guidelines and rules into his appraisal assignments and reports?

C. How might Larry stay abreast of regulatory agency guidelines considering the fact that such rules and regulations seem to be constantly changing?

Case 13

Ray completed an appraisal assignment six months ago for a group of out-of-town investors who said they were somewhat interested in developing a regional shopping mall on the outskirts of town. The site they had in mind was a 50-acre farm currently used to raise cattle. Ray completed the assignment, delivered the appraisal, and received his compensation. He never heard whether they decided to purchase the property.

Yesterday, a national fast-food chain contacted Ray in regard to its decision to locate three outlets in his town. The locations had already been "picked," although the chain had not contacted the owners of the property about selling. One of the spots picked was on the highway directly across from the 50-acre farm Ray appraised for the "proposed mall." Ray accepts the appraisal assignment from the fast-food chain.

A.   Should Ray accept this appraisal assignment?

B.   By accepting the second appraisal assignment has Ray violated any rules in the uniform standards? Explain.

C.   Is Ray obligated under the USPAP to inform the fast-food chain of the results of this previous appraisal?

Case 14

Beth is currently certified as a residential appraiser. She specializes in all types of one-to-four family residential property including condominiums. She also has appraised a time-share unit and recently completed a very competent appraisal for a four-unit apartment building. Because she has her "residential" designation from a well-known appraisal organization, she has decided to pursue an "income" designation and has, in fact, successfully completed one income capitalization course.

Beth has been contacted by an investor who is considering purchasing a 250-unit apartment complex in the city where Beth does most of her appraisal work. While she has never taken on an assignment of this magnitude, she is confident of her knowledge and has no doubt that she can complete the assignment. She accepts the assignment.

A.   Is Beth fulfilling the requirements of the Competency Rule when she accepts this assignment? If not, what should she do?

B.   Is Beth competent to accept this assignment? What if the apartment complex was only 50 units, rather than 250 units?

C.   By accepting this assignment, has she violated any provisions of the USPAP?

Case 15

Billy has just become a state certified general appraiser. Historically, he has spent most of his time appraising residential single-family property but has from time to time accepted an assignment to appraise rental property. Once, he appraised a 4-unit apartment complex. The owner of the local boat marina is interested in refinancing his project and asks Billy if he can help him. The owner goes on to ask Billy if he has ever appraised a marina. Because Billy has never appraised a boat marina, his response is, "No, but appraising is appraising, and I am competent I will do a good job for you. Besides, do you know what it would cost to bring in one of those experts from out of town?" The owner decides to employ Billy.

A. Should Billy accept this appraisal assignment?

B. If your answer to Question A is "yes," what makes Billy competent to accept the assignment?

C. How does the "knowledge and experience" criteria mentioned in the Competency Rule relate to the fact that the "world's expert" on appraising boat marinas had to appraise the first one at some point in time?

Case 16

Marshall has been appraising all types of property for more than 30 years. Since 1987, he has included a certification statement in all his appraisals stating "my analyses, opinions, and conclusions were developed, and this report has been prepared, in conformity with the Uniform Standards of Professional Appraisal Practice." He became state certified during 1990. However, in 2001, Marshall decided to retire. He sent letters to all of his clients explaining his intentions to retire and telling them that if they want their workfiles and appraisal reports to "let me know, because at the end of next month, it's all going in the dumpster." A few of Marshall's clients contact him and he sends them their workfiles. The majority of his clients, however, did not contact him.

A.   Because Marshall has retired, was he still obligated to save his workfiles? Explain.

B.   Since Marshall is now retired, is there any jurisdiction over him in case someone complains to the state appraisal board that Marshall did not keep his records as required by the USPAP?

C.   What would you suggest to Marshall?

Case 17

The majority of residential loans made in Smallville are financed by the First National Bank. Susan, a local certified residential appraiser, is known as being competent and conscientious in her appraisal assignments. Recently, the bank came under new management that included placing the loan underwriters on an incentive plan. They receive a sizable commission if, and only if, the loan is actually closed. Susan is told by the chief loan officer that beginning next month, the $350 appraisal fee she receives for each appraisal assignment will be paid only if the loan is closed. Because Susan must rely on her appraisal income, she decides to "go along with the decision." Really, there won't be any problem because the community is growing, residential values are increasing, and, in fact, the bank has not had a foreclosure during the previous five years.

    A.   Has Susan done anything wrong?

    B.   Has she violated any sections of the Ethics Rule?

    C.   What should Susan tell the financial institution in terms of her need to be in compliance with the USPAP?

Case 18

Martha is the owner of a five-person appraisal firm. She rents office space in a locally owned four-story office building. The owner has decided to sell the building. An investor from another city is interested in purchasing the building and during the initial visit, the investor notices Martha's offices. The investor contacts Martha and asks her to appraise the building for him because "who else would be in a better position to know what it is worth than an appraiser in the building?" The purpose of the appraisal report will be to estimate investment value. Martha accepts the appraisal assignment.

A.   Should Martha accept this appraisal assignment?

B.   If your answer to Question A is "no," why should she not accept it?

C.   Would there be conditions under which Martha could accept this assignment? Explain.

Case 19

First National Bank has used John's services to appraise both residential and commercial property throughout the city for the past 15 years. John's work has been satisfactory. The bank is currently in the midst of an audit being conducted by the Office of the Comptroller of the Currency (OCC). As part of the audit process, 30 of John's appraisals are randomly chosen. OCC auditors discover numerous spelling errors, typos, misnumbered pages and a few charts and tables out of place in some of John's appraisals. In addition, some math errors have been made, although in such instances the final value estimates were not impacted.

A.   How many "small errors" does it take before an appraiser is in violation of the USPAP? Explain.

B.   Does the USPAP require John to correct these errors and resubmit the appraisal reports?

C.   Would the institution have a legitimate complaint against John? Explain.

Case 20

Richard, a state certified appraiser, has a great deal of experience appraising proposed subdivision developments for developers as well as financial institutions. A subdivision on the outskirts of town has been under development for the past three years. While Richard did not appraise it, he is familiar with the location and some of the problems the developer has had. The insurance company that held the development loan has foreclosed on the subdivision, but because of some technicalities in the foreclosure statutes, the developer is suing the insurance company. The result of all the suits is that the whole matter is now before a judge. Richard is contacted by the court to see if he will appraise the property as a disinterested third party. Richard agrees. The judge, who knows a little bit about appraisals, reminds Richard that he is not to use the "subdivision or development method" of site valuation because the state supreme court recently ruled such a method was too speculative and thus inadmissible in a court of law.

A.   Can Richard accept the assignment and still be in compliance with the USPAP?

B.   Can Richard make an appraisal given the instructions of the judge and, if so, is Richard in violation of the USPAP if he follows the orders of the court?

C.   What does the USPAP say in regard to recognized appraisal methods not being used because of court decisions?

Case 21

Don, a general certified appraiser, is the owner of a successful appraisal/consulting firm. Five people work for him, all of whom are either licensed or residential certified. From time to time, Don receives a request from a developer/builder who needs someone to "work with him" in obtaining financing for a customer who wants to purchase a new home. When Don receives such a request, he gives the assignment to one of his employees. In fact, some of the time, the developer/builder calls one of the licensed appraisers directly and does not even run it by Don. The assignments are always completed on time. Don only signs the reports and forwards them to the developer/builder. Don receives the fee and gives one-half of it to the person who actually did the appraisal.

A. Has Don violated any of the provisions of the Ethics Rule? If the answer is "yes," what has he violated?

B. If your answer to Question A is "yes," would your answer have been the same if Don did not sign the report? Explain.

C. If your answer to Question A is "yes," would your answer have been the same if Don did not receive any of the fee? Explain.

Case 22

Joe is a review appraiser for the state highway department and as such spends the majority of his time reviewing the appraisal reports completed by fee appraisers. The appraisal he has just read involves an opinion as to the market value of a large tract of land that is part of an eminent domain proceeding. Joe has information that leads him to conclude the appraised value reported in the appraisal is considerably less than what it should be. So as not to "embarrass" the fee appraiser, Joe simply puts his higher value opinion on the review report without any explanation as to how the higher number was derived. When questioned by his supervisor concerning why he took such an approach, Joe responded that as a review appraiser, he did not have to explain or justify his actions and furthermore, "I am not in violation of the uniform standards."

A.   Is Joe in violation of the USPAP? Explain.

B.   If Joe is in violation of the USPAP, as a review appraiser what should he have done if he disagreed with the estimate of value?

Case 23

Marti, a well-respected residential appraiser, completed the appraisal of a ten-acre tract of land that included a home two years ago. Recently, the present owner, the same person who employed Marti, decided to sell the property. During the title search, a written, recorded easement that gave access to a neighbor across the property was discovered. The owner did not know the easement existed and in fact had just assumed the neighbor was using the property in question. The owner really did not care because no harm had been done. Marti was contacted and asked why she did not point out the existence of the easement in her appraisal report. Marti's response was that she was not responsible for questions of a legal matter, and while she would admit that this easement would indeed have an impact on value, the presence of an easement should have been made known to her when the appraisal assignment was given.

A. Is Marti in violation of any rules of the USPAP?

B. Does the USPAP require the appraiser to render any legal opinion? Explain.

C. Could/should Marti have included a statement in her limiting conditions section that would cover her omission of the easement in the appraisal report?

Case 24

Bryant, a certified general appraiser, is in the midst of completing all of the requirements for his "income-property" designation to be awarded by a national professional appraisal organization. The last step in the process requires a professional peer review committee to review some of Bryant's work and meet with him to discuss his assignments. Because the majority of what Bryant would refer to as his "best appraisals" are done for only one client, Bryant has a problem. This particular client, who happens to be an international investor, insists that all appraisal work done for him shall remain confidential. In fact, Bryant has signed an agreement with the investor that none of the information contained in any of the appraisals will be made available to anyone—no exceptions. Bryant knows that if he does not use some of his "better appraisals," there is no chance of the peer review committee recommending that he be awarded the designation.

A. According to the USPAP, must Bryant show his work to a professional peer review committee?

B. If he refuses to give the professional peer review committee the appraisals, has Bryant violated any rule of the USPAP?

C. According to the USPAP, what should Bryant do?

D. If copies of Bryant's appraisals are given to members of the professional peer review committee, what obligation, if any, do committee members have to Bryant?

Case 25

Gerald is considered the guru of waterfront industrial property along the eastern seaboard. He travels extensively along the Atlantic coast and is familiar with most of the large industrial properties in the area. Gerald is contacted by an insurance company that has used his appraisal services before. The insurance company has a contract pending on an industrial warehouse if "we can have an appraisal within three days for at least $1,200,000." They tell Gerald that they know his services are expensive, but "if you can do it, we will pay you $20,000." Gerald assures them that he will have no problem coming up with a number at least equal to $1,200,000 and he accepts the assignment. The next day he receives an overnight package containing a letter of engagement and a check payable to him for $20,000.

A. Is the $20,000 a contingency fee? Explain.

B. Given the directive by the client that the company needs the work "within three days for at least $1,200,000," can Gerald accept the assignment?

C. What should Gerald do to comply with the USPAP?

Case 26

Ken is interested in financing a house. He visits a local financial institution and the loan officer hands Ken a list of the local approved appraisers. Ken is told to pick someone to do the appraisal, have the appraiser make the appraisal out to the lender and then pay the appraiser whatever she charges. Ken hires an appraiser on the approved list and orders the appraisal. The appraiser subsequently completes the report and sends the report to the loan officer. The appraiser is paid by Ken. The appraisal report conforms to the requirements of the USPAP.

A.   Has the appraiser violated the USPAP?

B.   If your answer to Question A is "yes," what rules have been violated?

C.   What should the appraiser have done? Explain.

Case 27

Morris is a certified general appraiser in Dallas, Texas, and is considered to be an expert in the appraisal of industrial warehouses. He is asked to appraise an industrial warehouse in Laughlin, Nevada. Even though he has never been in Laughlin, Nevada, Morris accepts the assignment and completes the appraisal.

A.   Has Morris violated the USPAP? Explain.

B.   If Morris accepts the assignment, what could he do to protect himself from recoursse by the client?

Case 28

Two months ago an appraiser completed an appraisal assignment for a financial institution in regard to the financing of a house. The appraiser was paid but due to other circumstances the deal fell through. Yesterday the original borrower went to a second lender to seek financing. The second lender contacts the appraiser and instructs the appraiser to simply "readdress the URAR to me" or else "send me a new cover letter along with the old URAR." The second lender informs the appraiser that the appraiser will be sent $100 for her efforts.

A.   If the appraiser does as instructed has she violated the USPAP? Explain.

B.   Must the appraiser readdress the appraisal to the second lender?

Case 29

A lender requested you to complete an evaluation for the purpose of making a $25,000 home improvement loan. Currently there is a $150,000 first mortgage on the property. You complete the evaluation and deliver it to the lender.

    A.   Have you violated any of the rules of the USPAP? If the answer is "yes," what have you violated and why?

    B.   Do "evaluations" fall under state appraisal statutes?

Case 30

Steve recently completed an appraisal assignment for a bank and was paid by the bank. The bank subsequently gave a copy of the appraisal to the borrower. Steve had included in his limiting conditions statement that no one could be given a copy of the appraisal without his written permission.

A.   Can the bank give a copy of the appraisal without Steve's permission? Explain.

B.   If the bank gives the borrower a copy of the appraisal report, is Steve now obligated to answer questions he receives directly from the borrower?

Examination I

Examination I covers subjects from the Preamble and Rules Section through Standard 3 of the USPAP as well as a general overview of the remaining standards. You should not attempt to answer these questions until you have studied the sections of the USPAP covered in this book and feel comfortable with the material. Completion of both examinations in this book should be considered excellent preparation for any examination you will be taking on the uniform standards.

Examination I

1. The definition of market value in the USPAP Glossary is based on a number of conditions. Which of the following conditions are assumed?

   A. The buyer and the seller are atypically motivated.
   B. Neither party is well informed.
   C. All parties are acting in what they consider their best interests.
   D. A maximum time is allowed for exposure in the open market.

2. Standard 2 addresses the need for the appraiser to place the assumptions and limiting conditions in an identified section of the appraisal report. Which of the following statements is an example of an assumption of limiting condition?

   A. "My analyses, opinions, and conclusions were developed, and this report has been prepared, in conformity with the Uniform Standards of Professional Appraisal Practice."
   B. "My engagement in this assignment was not contingent upon developing or reporting predetermined results."
   C. "On all appraisals, subject to satisfactory completion, repairs, or alterations, the appraisal report and value conclusion are contingent on completion of the improvements in a workmanlike manner."
   D. "No one provided significant professional assistance to the person signing this report."

3. In regard to the Record Keeping Section of the Ethics Rule, which of the following statements is correct?

    A. An appraiser must prepare a workfile for each assignment.

    B. A workfile does not have to be made available by the appraiser when required by due process of law.

    C. The five-year and two-year periods are maximums.

    D. Oral testimony is not subject to the record keeping requirements.

4. Standard 9 addresses the development of what type of appraisal assignment?

    A. Real Property

    B. Personal Property

    C. Mass Appraisal

    D. Business Appraisal

5. If prior to accepting an appraisal assignment, an appraiser believes that she does not have the knowledge and experience to complete the assignment competently, she must do three things. Which of the following actions must be done?

    A. Disclose the lack of knowledge and/or experience to the client before accepting the assignment but only if the client inquires.

    B. Take all the steps necessary or appropriate to complete the assignment competently.

    C. If the subject is income producing property, describe the lack of knowledge and/or experience and the steps taken to complete the assignment competently in the report.

    D. Document in the appraisal report that the state appraisal board ruled that she was competent to complete the assignment.

6. The standards and the standards rules are followed by "comments." Which of the following statements is correct in regard to these comments?

    A. Comments are not an integral part of the USPAP, but rather are the personal opinions of the members of the ASB.

    B. Comments should be disregarded if they are part of a specific requirement.

    C. Comments provide interpretation from the ASB concerning the background and application of certain rules, definitions or standards rules.

    D. Additional comments have not been added since the uniform standards have never been changed and cannot be changed.

7.   The Definitions Section of the USPAP references an appraisal practice by three terms. Appraisal practice, as defined, includes

    A.   market analysis.
    B.   appraisal brokerage activities.
    C.   appraisal consulting.
    D.   investment analysis.

8.   An appraisal report must contain certain minimum requirements as per Standards Rule 2-2. Which of the following items is required (as a minimum) to be included in every appraisal report?

    A.   Intended use of the appraisal
    B.   Name of previous owners
    C.   Definition of market value
    D.   Effective date of the expected title transfer

9.   The reporting of the results of a personal property appraisal by an appraiser is the subject matter of which standard?

    A.   Standard 2
    B.   Standard 5
    C.   Standard 8
    D.   Standard 10

10.   An appraiser must retain his or her records for a period of at least _____ years after preparation, or at least _____ years after final disposition of any judicial proceeding in which testimony was given, whichever period expires last.

    A.   two years; two years
    B.   two years; five years
    C.   five years; two years
    D.   five years; five years

11.   There are four sections that make up the Ethics Rule. Which of the following activities is a section of the Ethics Rule?

    A.   Preamble
    B.   Departure
    C.   Jurisdictional Exception
    D.   Confidentiality

12.   Even though important, which of the following "products" of the ASB has the least direct inpact on an appraiser?

        A.   Advisory opinions
        B.   Statements on standards
        C.   Standards rules
        D.   Standards

13.   Which of the following statements is correct in regard to contingency compensation?

        A.   The acceptance of compensation contingent on the reporting of a predetermined value in an appraisal is unethical.
        B.   Contingency fees are addressed in the Record Keeping Section of the Ethics Rule.
        C.   Restrictions on contingency compensation do not apply to appraisal review assignments where the review appraiser did not conduct the original appraisal.
        D.   Contingency compensation in an appraisal consulting practice is ethical.

14.   According to the Definitions of the uniform standards, the purpose of many real property appraisal assignments is to render an opinion of

        A.   investment value.
        B.   market value.
        C.   loan value.
        D.   likely sales price.

15.   Standard 2 addresses the certification statement prepared by the person signing the appraisal report. In regard to that certification, which one of the following statements is correct?

        A.   The suggestion that the appraisal report contain a certification statement is a specific requirement rather than a binding requirement.
        B.   The statement should say that the subject property has been personally inspected by the person signing the report.
        C.   The name of each individual providing clerical assistance must be stated.
        D.   The statement should say the report was prepared in conformity with the USPAP.

16. According to the Confidentiality Section of the Ethics Rule, certain persons may have confidential factual data from an appraisal assignment disclosed to them. Which of the following persons is clearly recognized under the Confidentiality Section?

    A. All persons who read the appraisal report
    B. Appraisers who had previously valued the property
    C. Parties authorized under due process of law
    D. All members of the appraiser's local appraisal organization

17. In regard to considering and analyzing any current agreement of sale of the property being appraised, which of the following statements is correct?

    A. The time frames cited are maximums.
    B. The intent of the requirement is to encourage research and analysis.
    C. All previous sales agreements within the stated time frames must, without exception, be examined.
    D. The time period for one-to-four family residential property is longer than for other property types.

18. Which standard is directed toward the substantive aspects of developing a competent appraisal of real property?

    A. Standard 1
    B. Standard 2
    C. Standard 4
    D. Standard 5

19. The Definitions Section of the uniform standards would classify an item such as furnishings or machinery and equipment as

    A. real property.
    B. personal property.
    C. personal estate.
    D. real estate.

20.   Since 1991, the ASB has added statements on standards to the USPAP. Which of the following statements is correct in regard to statements on standards?

    A.   Statements on standards change standards and standards rules.
    B.   Statements on standards do not have the same weight as standards rules.
    C.   Statements on standards serve to clarify, interpret, explain and elaborate on the USPAP.
    D.   Statements on standards can only be adopted by certified appraisers.

21.   An appraiser decides to perform a limited appraisal assignment that calls for something less than the work required by the specific requirements. What should the appraiser do?

    A.   Always refer to the finished product as a consulting assignment.
    B.   Base his or her compensation on a contingency fee.
    C.   Only report the results on a form appraisal report.
    D.   Clearly set forth this fact in the report.

22.   The performance of a real estate or real property consulting service by an appraiser is the subject matter of which standard?

    A.   Standard 1
    B.   Standard 4
    C.   Standard 7
    D.   Standard 9

23.   The USPAP defines the act or process of developing and communicating an opinion about the quality of another appraiser's work as a(n)

    A.   appraisal review.
    B.   appraisal.
    C.   appraisal report.
    D.   appraisal consulting assignment.

24.   Standard 1 requires, as a minimum, that an appraiser must consider and analyze any prior sales of the property being appraised for one-to-four family residential property for a minimum period of

    A.   one year.
    B.   two years.
    C.   three years.
    D.   five years.

25.   According to the definitions in the USPAP, "a study that reflects the relationship between acquisition price and anticipated future benefits of a real estate investment" is referred to as a(n)

    A.   cash flow analysis.
    B.   feasibility analysis.
    C.   investment analysis.
    D.   market analysis.

Examination II

Examination II covers subjects from the Preamble and Rules Section through Standard 3 of the USPAP as well as a general overview of the remaining standards. You should not attempt to answer these questions until you have studied the sections of the USPAP covered in this book and feel comfortable with the material. Completion of both examinations in this book should be considered excellent preparation for any examination you will be taking on the uniform standards.

Examination II

1.   The Ethics Rule contains four sections. Which of the following activities is part of the Ethics Rule?

    A.   Confidentiality
    B.   Departure
    C.   Jurisdictional Exception
    D.   Competency

2.   In regard to the Preamble of the USPAP, which of the following statements is correct?

    A.   The USPAP reflects the current standards of the appraisal profession.
    B.   The USPAP was developed by the Appraisal Subcommittee for the purpose of regulating appraisers.
    C.   The standards include Advisory Opinions which are part of the standards.
    D.   The standards deal with the procedures to be followed in performing an appraisal or appraisal review, but not a consulting service.

3. In regard to the certification statement required in each written real property appraisal report, which one of the following statements is correct?

    A. If anyone provided significant real property appraisal assistance to the person signing the report, the appraiser signing the report may want to include his or her name.
    B. The appraiser signing the report must certify that he or she personally inspected the subject property.
    C. The appraiser must certify that his or her compensation is contingent on the reporting of a predetermined value that favors the cause of the client.
    D. The appraiser should state whether he or she has any present or prospective interest in the property that is the subject of the report.

4. The definition of market value in the USPAP Glossary is based on a number of conditions. Which of the following conditions is assumed?

    A. A long time is allowed for exposure in the open market
    B. Both parties are uninformed
    C. The price does not include any special financing to which the seller agrees
    D. The buyer and the seller are typically motivated

5. According to the USPAP, which provision or standard states that "in reporting the results of a real property appraisal, an appraiser must communicate each analysis, opinion, and conclusion in a manner that is not misleading?"

    A. Standard 1
    B. Standard 2
    C. Standard 3
    D. Standard 5

6. The Definitions Section of the USPAP would classify an item such as land as

    A. real estate.
    B. real property.
    C. personal property.
    D. fixture.

7.   According to Standard 2, an appraiser who signs any part of the appraisal report, including a letter of transmittal, must also:

     A.   be a certified general appraiser.
     B.   personally inspect the property before signing the report.
     C.   receive at least 50 percent of the appraisal fee.
     D.   sign the certification.

8.   "Having the knowledge and experience necessary to complete the assignment" is part of the

     A.   Departure Rule.
     B.   Ethics Rule.
     C.   Jurisdictional Exception Rule.
     D.   Competency Rule.

9.   Standard 2 requires the appraiser to clearly and accurately disclose any extraordinary assumptions or limiting conditions that directly affect the appraisal and indicate the impact these conditions have on value. Which of the following conditions would be an example of such activity?

     A.   Execution of a personal property bill of sale for one of the comps.
     B.   Revocation of an appraiser's certification by the appraisal board.
     C.   Atypical financing of the properties in the neighborhood.
     D.   Completion of offsite improvements.

10. The USPAP defines appraisal consulting as

     A.   the act or process of estimating value.
     B.   the act or process of critically studying a report prepared by another.
     C.   the act or process of developing an analysis, recommendation or opinion to solve a problem where an opinion of value is a component of the analysis leading to the assignment results.
     D.   the process of valuing a universe of properties.

11. The reporting of the results of a real estate or real property consulting service by an appraiser is the subject matter of which standard?

     A.   Standard 2
     B.   Standard 5
     C.   Standard 8
     D.   Standard 10

12. Which of the following statements is correct in regard to the certification statement required in each written real property appraisal report?

    A. The statement must be in a separate section of the appraisal report.
    B. The statement must follow the specific wording as detailed in Standards Rule 2-3.
    C. The statement should say whether the subject property was personally inspected.
    D. The inclusion of a certification statement is a specific requirement.

13. In regard to considering and analyzing any current agreement of sale of the property being appraised, which of the following statements is correct?

    A. This specific requirement does permit departure.
    B. The information, if available to the appraiser in the normal course of business, must be analyzed.
    C. The time frames cited in the requirement are maximums.
    D. The minimum period of time to be covered for all property types is three years.

14. On July 1, 1996, an appraiser prepares an appraisal report for the taking of a parcel of land through eminent domain. The proceedings lead to court action and the dispute is settled in court on July 1, 2001. As a minimum, the appraiser must retain his or her records/reports until:

    A. July 1, 1996.
    B. July 1, 2001.
    C. July 1, 2003.
    D. July 1, 2006.

15. Which of the following statements is correct in regard to the standards rules?

    A. Standards rules are much shorter than the standards.
    B. Standards rules are more specific in direction than the standards.
    C. None of the standards rules are followed by explanatory comments.
    D. Departure from the standards rules is not permitted.

16.   According to the definitions included in the uniform standards, the work or services performed in valuation services are defined by three terms. Which of the following terms is used to define an appraisal practice?

    A.   Evaluator
    B.   Appraiser Counseling
    C.   Fee Negotiator
    D.   Appraisal Consulting

17.   According to the definitions in the USPAP, "a study of market conditions for a specific type of property" is referred to as a(an)

    A.   cash flow analysis.
    B.   feasibility analysis.
    C.   investment analysis.
    D.   market analysis.

18.   Standard 2 addresses the application and use of the traditional approaches to value. In terms of how the approaches to value are used, which of the following statements best describes what Standards Rule 2-2(a) requires for a self-contained appraisal report?

    A.   If the appraisal report concerns residential property, the sales comparison approach must have been used.
    B.   The appraiser must justify the use of any approach used in the report.
    C.   The appraiser must explain and support the reason for excluding any of the usual valuation approaches.
    D.   One of the usual approaches cannot be eliminated simply because the data collected does not support the use of that approach.

19.   The Ethics Rule contains four sections. Which of the following sections is part of the Ethics Rule?

    A.   Preamble
    B.   Competency
    C.   Management
    D.   Supplemental Standards

20.   The Competency Rule requires that if facts or conditions are uncovered during the course of an assignment that cause the appraiser to believe that he or she lacks the required experience to complete the assignment competently, the appraiser must complete three steps. Which of the following steps is specifically mentioned in the rule?

    A.   Automatically withdrawing from the appraisal assignment.
    B.   Notifying the property owner of the lack of experience.
    C.   Taking the steps necessary or appropriate to complete the assignment.
    D.   Describing the lack of experience but not the steps taken to complete the assignment competently.

21.   "The act or process of developing and communicating an opinion about the quality of another appraiser's work is referred to as a(n)

    A.   appraisal review.
    B.   report.
    C.   analysis, opinion and conclusion.
    D.   review.

22.   The development of a personal property appraisal is the subject matter of which standard?

    A.   Standard 1
    B.   Standard 4
    C.   Standard 7
    D.   Standard 9

23.   Periodically, the ASB issues "advisory opinions" as well as publishing statements on standards. In regard to advisory opinions and statements on standards, which of the following comments is correct?

    A.   Advisory opinions establish new standards.
    B.   Statements on standards do not have the same weight as standards rules.
    C.   Advisory opinions are enforceable against appraisers.
    D.   Statements on standards serve to clarify, interpret, explain and elaborate the USPAP.

24. Standard 1 requires, as a minimum, an appraiser to examine any current agreements of sale for all property types other than one-to-four family residential property for a period of

    A.   one year.
    B.   two years.
    C.   three years.
    D.   five years.

25. Standard 10 addresses the reporting of what type of appraisal assignments?

    A.   Real property
    B.   Personal property
    C.   Mass appraisal
    D.   Business appraisal

Appendix A

Uniform Standards of

Professional Appraisal Practice*

(Introduction—Standard 3)

UNIFORM STANDARDS OF PROFESSIONAL APPRAISAL PRACTICE

2002 Edition

Effective: January 1, 2002 - December 31, 2002

FOREWORD

The Appraisal Standards Board (ASB) of The Appraisal Foundation develops, publishes, interprets and amends the Uniform Standards of Professional Appraisal Practice (USPAP) on behalf of appraisers and users of appraisal services. Since USPAP will be used by state and federal regulatory agencies and others, the ASB has adopted a publication policy to ensure that everyone is informed of interpretations of or amendments to USPAP in a regular and timely manner. The 2002 edition is the eleventh annual publication of USPAP.

The ASB publishes the USPAP in an annual bound edition that includes: a history of any changes during the prior year. This 2002 edition of USPAP is divided into three sections: "PREAMBLE", STANDARDS AND STANDARDS RULES", and STATEMENTS ON APPRAISAL STANDARDS".

In addition, for convenience of reference, this bound volume also contains Advisory Opinions and a Glossary approved by the ASB and an Index. These reference materials are a form of "Other Communications" provided by the ASB for guidance only and are not an integral part of USPAP.

It is important that individuals understand and adhere to changes in each annual edition of USPAP. This edition becomes effective **January 1, 2002.** State and Federal regulatory authorities enforce the content of the current edition of USPAP.

Origin and History of USPAP

These standards are based on the original Uniform Standards of Professional Appraisal Practice developed in 1986-87 by the Ad Hoc Committee on Uniform Standards and copyrighted in 1987 by The Appraisal Foundation. Prior to the establishment of the ASB in 1989, the USPAP had been adopted by major appraisal organizations in North America and became recognized as the generally accepted standards of appraisal practice.

At its organizational meeting on January 30, 1989, the Appraisal Standards Board of The Appraisal Foundation unanimously approved and adopted the original USPAP as the initial appraisal standards promulgated by the ASB. The USPAP may be altered, amended, interpreted, supplemented, or repealed by the ASB after exposure to the appraisal profession, users of appraisal services and the public in accordance with established rules of procedure.

Effective Date of Original Uniform Standards: April 27, 1987

Amendments by the Appraisal Standards Board to Date; excluding administrative edits made in 1999:

Preamble	September 15, 1999
Ethics Rule	September 16, 1998
Competency Rule	September 15, 1999
Departure Rule	September 16, 1998
Jurisdictional Exception and Supplemental Standards Rules	July 19, 1994
Definitions	September 15, 1999
Standard 1	September 15, 1999
Standard 2	September 15, 1999
Standard 3	June 5, 1990
Standards 4 and 5	September 10, 1991
Standard 6	September 15, 1999
Standards 7 and 8	September 15, 1999
Standards 9 and 10	

Statements on Appraisal Standards:

Statements on Appraisal Standards are authorized by the by-laws of The Appraisal Foundation and are specifically for the purpose of clarification, interpretation, explanation or elaboration of USPAP. Statements have the full weight of a Standard Rule and can only by adopted by the ASB after exposure and comment. To date the ASB has adopted nine Statements and retired one. The dates listed below are the dates they were adopted or retired.

SMT-1	Standards Rule 3-1 (f)(Review Appraisal)	July 8, 1991; retired September 15, 1999
SMT-2	Discounted Cash Flow Analysis	July 8, 1991
SMT-3	Retrospective Value Estimates	July 8, 1991
SMT-4	Prospective Value Estimates	July 8, 1991
SMT-5	Confidentiality Rule of the Ethics Provision	September 10, 1991; retired July 1, 2001
SMT-6	Reasonable Exposure Time in Market Value Estimates	September 16, 1992
SMT-7	Permitted Departure from Specific Guidelines for Real Property Appraisals	March 22, 1994
SMT-8	Electronic Transmission of Reports	July 18, 1995; retired July 1, 2001
SMT-9	Identification of the Client's "Intended Use" in Developing and Reporting Appraisal, Consulting or Review Assignment Opinions and Conclusions	August 27, 1996
SMT-10	Assignments for Use by a Federally Insured Depository Institution in a Federally Related Transaction	July 1, 2000 ; July 1, 2001

Advisory Opinions

In addition to Statements on Appraisal Standards, the ASB also issues Advisory Opinions. This type of communication by the ASB does not establish new standards or interpret existing standards. Advisory Opinions do not constitute legal opinions of the ASB. Advisory Opinions are issued to illustrate the applicability of appraisal standards in specific situations and to offer advice from the ASB for the resolution of appraisal issues and problems. To date the ASB has adopted the following Advisory Opinions for general distribution:

AO-1	Sales History	December 3, 1990
AO-2	Inspection of Subject Property Real Estate	December 4, 1990***
AO-3	Update of an Appraisal	March 5, 1991****
AO-4	Standards Rule 1-5(b)	June 3, 1991***
AO-5	Assistance in the Preparation of an Appraisal	May 1, 1992****
AO-6	The Appraisal Review Function	June 2, 1992****
AO-7	Marketing Time Estimates	September 16, 1992****
AO-8	Market Value vs. Fair Value in Real Property Appraisals	September 16, 1992****
AO-9	Responsibility of Appraisers Concerning Toxic or Hazardous Substance Contamination	December 8, 1992***
AO-10	The Appraiser-Client Relationship	March 23, 1993****
AO-11	Content of the Appraisal Report Options of Standards Rule 2-2 and 2-8	July 20, 1994****
AO-12	Use of the Appraisal Report Options of Standard 2	July 20, 1994****
AO-13	Performing Evaluations of Real Property Collateral to Conform with USPAP	July 18, 1995***
AO-14	Appraisals for Subsidized Housing	July 19, 1995***
AO-15	Using the Departure Provision in Developing a Limited Appraisal	July 26, 1996****
AO-16	Fair Housing Laws and Appraisal Report Content	June 10, 1996***
AO-17	Appraisals of Real Property with Proposed Improvements	July 26, 1996***

AO-18 Use of an Automated Valuation Model (AVM)   July 9, 1997***
AO-19 Unacceptable Assignment Conditions in Real Property Appraisal Assignments   September 15, 1999
AO-20 An Appraisal Review Assignment That Includes the Reviewer's Own
      Opinion of Value   January 1, 2001
AO-21 When Does USPAP Apply in Valuation Services?   January 1, 2001
AO-22 Scope of Work in Market Value Appraisal Assignments, Real Property   January 1, 2001
AO-23 Identifying the Relevant Characteristics of the Subject Property of a Real
      Property Appraisal Assignment   January 1, 2001

   *   *revised May 25, 1993 and March 22, 1994*
  **   *revised March 25, 1996*
 ***   *revised September 16, 1998*
**** *revised September 15, 1999*

The 1992, 1993, 1994 and 1995 Editions of USPAP included a mid-year supplement. In order to clarify public understanding of the effective dates of USPAP revisions, Statements and Advisory Opinions , in 1995 the ASB elected to discontinue the mid-year supplement of the 1996 Edition and all subsequent editions.

The Appraisal Standards Board develops and amends appraisal standards through communications with appraisers and users of appraisal services. If you have any comments, questions, or suggestions regarding USPAP, please contact the ASB.

Appraisal Standards Board
The Appraisal Foundation
1029 Vermont Avenue, NW
Suite 900
Washington, D.C. 20005-3517
Phone: (202) 347-7722
FAX: (202) 347-7727
www.appraisalfoundation.org

TABLE OF CONTENTS

UNIFORM STANDARDS OF PROFESSIONAL APPRAISAL PRACTICE

PREAMBLE
ETHICS RULE
COMPETENCY RULE
DEPARTURE RULE
JURISDICTIONAL EXCEPTION RULE
SUPPLEMENTAL STANDARDS RULE
DEFINITIONS

STANDARDS AND STANDARDS RULES

STATEMENTS ON APPRAISAL STANDARDS

ADVISORY OPINIONS

GLOSSARY

INDEX

UNIFORM STANDARDS OF
PROFESSIONAL APPRAISAL PRACTICE

as promulgated by the
Appraisal Standards Board of
The Appraisal Foundation

PREAMBLE

The purpose of these Standards is to establish requirements for professional appraisal practice, which includes appraisal, consulting and review, as defined. The intent of these Standards is to promote and maintain a high level of public trust in professional appraisal practice.

These standards are for appraisers and users of appraisal services. To maintain a high level of professional practice, appraisers observe these Standards. However, these Standards do not in themselves establish which individuals or assignments must comply; neither the Appraisal Foundation nor its Appraisal Standards Board are government entities with the power to make, judge or enforce law. Individuals comply with these Standards either by choice or by requirements placed upon them, or upon the service they provide, by law, regulation, or agreement with the client or intended users to comply.

It is essential that professional appraisers develop and communicate their analyses, opinions, and conclusions to intended users of their services in a manner that will be meaningful and not misleading. These *Uniform Standards of Professional Appraisal Practice* reflect the current standards of the appraisal profession.

The importance of the role of the appraiser places ethical obligations on those who serve in this capacity. These standards include explanatory Comments and begin with an ETHICS RULE setting forth the requirements for integrity, impartiality, objectivity, independent judgment, and ethical conduct. In addition, these Standards include a COMPETENCY RULE which places an immediate responsibility on the appraiser prior to acceptance of an assignment as well as during the performance of an assignment. DEFINITIONS applicable to these Standards are also included. The Standards contain binding requirements, as well as specific requirements to which the DEPARTURE RULE may apply under certain conditions. No departure is permitted from the PREAMBLE, ETHICS RULE, COMPETENCY RULE or DEFINITIONS section.

These standards deal with the procedures to be followed in performing an appraisal, review or consulting service and the manner in which an appraisal, review or consulting service is communicated. STANDARDS 1 and 2 establish requirements for the development and communication of a real property appraisal. STANDARD 3 establishes requirements for reviewing a real property appraisal and reporting on that review. STANDARDS 4 and 5 establish requirements for the development and communication of various real estate or real property consulting functions by an appraiser. STANDARD 6 establishes requirements for the development and reporting of mass appraisals for ad valorem tax purposes or any other universe of properties. STANDARDS 7 and 8 establish requirements for developing and communicating personal property appraisals. STANDARDS 9 and 10 establish requirements for developing and communicating business appraisals.

These Standards include Statements on Appraisal Standards issued by the Appraisal Standards Board for the purpose of clarification, interpretation, explanation, or elaboration of a Standard or Standards Rule.

PREAMBLE (continued)

> Comment: Comments are an integral part of the Uniform Standards and are extensions of the Definitions, and Standards Rules. Comments provide interpretation from the Appraisal Standards Board concerning the background or application of certain Rules, Definitions, or Standards Rules. Comments also establish the context of certain requirements and the conditions that apply only in specific situations or type of assignments.

> Footnotes referring to Advisory Opinions do not incorporate the Advisory Opinions into the *Uniform Standards of Professional Appraisal Practice.*

ETHICS RULE

To promote and preserve the public trust inherent in professional appraisal practice, an appraiser must observe the highest standards of professional ethics. This ETHICS RULE is divided into four sections: Conduct, Management, Confidentiality, and Record Keeping: the first three sections apply to all appraisal practice and all four sections apply to appraisal practice performed under Standards 1 through 10.

> Comment: This rule specifies the personal obligations and responsibilities of the individual appraiser. However, it should also be noted that groups and organizations engaged in appraisal practice share the same ethical obligations.

Compliance with these standards is required when either the service or the appraiser is obligated by law or regulation, or by an agreement with the client or intended users to comply. Compliance is also required when an individual, by choice, represents that he or she is performing the service as an appraiser.

An appraiser must not misrepresent his or her role when providing valuation services that are outside of appraisal practice.

> Comment: Honesty, impartiality, and professional competency are required of all appraisers under these *Uniform Standards of Professional Appraisal Practice* (USPAP). To document recognition and acceptance of his or her USPAP-related responsibilities in communicating an appraisal, appraisal review, or appraisal consulting assignment completed under USPAP, an appraiser is required to certify compliance with these Standards. (see Standards Rules 2-3, 3-3, 5-3, 6-8, 8-3 and 10-3).

Conduct

An appraiser must perform ethically and competently in accordance with these standards and must not engage in criminal conduct. An appraiser must perform assignments with impartiality, objectivity, and independence and without accommodation of personal interests.

In appraisal practice, an appraiser must not perform as an advocate for any party or issue.

> Comment: An appraiser may be an advocate only in support of his or her assignment results. Advocacy in any other form in appraisal practice is a violation of the ETHICS RULE.

An appraiser must not accept an assignment which includes the reporting of predetermined opinions and conclusions.

An appraiser must not communicate assignment results in a misleading or fraudulent manner. An appraiser must not use or communicate a misleading or fraudulent report or to knowingly permit an employee or other person to communicate a misleading or fraudulent report.

ETHICS RULE (continued)

An appraiser must not use or rely on unsupported conclusions relating to characteristics such as race, color, religion, national origin, gender, marital status, familial status, age, receipt of public assistance income, handicap, or an unsupported conclusion that homogeneity of such characteristics is necessary to maximize value.

> Comment: An individual appraiser employed by a group or organization which conducts itself in a manner that does not conform to these standards should take steps that are appropriate under the circumstances to ensure compliance with the standards.

Management

The payment of undisclosed fees, commissions, or things of value in connection with the procurement of appraisal, review, or consulting assignments is unethical.

> Comment: Disclosure of fees, commissions, or things of value connected to the procurement of an assignment should appear in the certification of a written report and in any transmittal letter in which conclusions are stated. In groups or organizations engaged in appraisal practice, intra-company payments to employees for business development are not considered to be unethical. Competency, rather than financial incentives, should be the primary basis for awarding an assignment.

It is unethical for the appraiser to accept compensation for performing an assignment when the assignment results are contingent upon:

1. **the reporting of a predetermined result(e.g., opinion of value), or**
2. **a direction in value that favors the cause of the client, or**
3. **the amount of the value opinion, or**
4. **the attainment of a stipulated result, or**
5. **the occurrence of a subsequent event directly related to the appraiser's opinions and specific to the assignment's purpose.**

Advertising for or soliciting appraisal assignments in a manner which is false, misleading, or exaggerated is unethical.

> Comment: In groups or organizations engaged in appraisal practice, decisions concerning finder or referral fees, contingent compensation, and advertising may not be the responsibility of an individual appraiser, but for a particular assignment, it is the responsibility of the individual appraiser to ascertain that there has been no breach of ethics, that the appraisal is prepared in accordance with these Standards, and that the report can be properly certified as required by Standard Rules 2-3, 3-2, 5-3, 6-8,8-3, or 10-3.

Confidentiality

An appraiser must protect the confidential nature of the appraiser-client relationship.

An appraiser must act in good faith with regard to the legitimate interests of the client in the use of confidential information and in the communication of assignment results.

An appraiser must be aware of, and comply with, all confidentiality and privacy laws and regulations applicable in an assignment.

ETHICS RULE (continued)

An appraiser must not disclose confidential information or assignment results prepared for a client to anyone other than the client and persons specifically authorized by the client; state enforcement agencies and such third parties as may be authorized by due process of law; and a duly authorized professional peer review committee except when such disclosure to a committee would violate applicable law or regulation. It is unethical for a member of a duly authorized professional peer review committee to disclose confidential information of factual data presented to the committee.

> Comment: When all confidential elements of confidential information are removed through redaction or the process of aggregation, client authorization is not required for the disclosure of the remaining information, as modified.

Record Keeping

An appraiser must prepare a workfile for each assignment. The workfile must include the name of the client and the identity, by name or type, of any other intended users; true copies of any written reports, documented on any type of media; summaries of any oral reports or testimony, or a transcript of testimony, including the appraiser's signed and dated certification; all other data, information and documentation necessary to support the appraiser's opinions and conclusions and to show compliance with this rule and all other applicable Standards, or references to the location(s) of such other documentation.

An appraiser must retain the workfile for a period of at least five (5) years after preparation or at least two (2) years after final disposition of any judicial proceeding in which testimony was given, whichever period expires last; and have custody of his other workfile, or make appropriate workfile retention, access and retrieval arrangements with the party having custody of the workfile.

> Comment: A workfile preserves evidence of the appraiser's consideration of all applicable data and statements required by USPAP and other information as may be required to support the findings and conclusions of the appraiser. For example, the content of a workfile for a Complete Appraisal must reflect consideration of all USPAP requirements applicable to the specific Complete Appraisal assignment. However, the content of a workfile for a Limited Appraisal need only reflect consideration of the USPAP requirements from which there has been no departure and that are required to the specific Limited Appraisal assignment.
>
> A photocopy or an electronic copy of the entire actual written appraisal, review, or consulting report sent or delivered to a client satisfies the requirement of a true copy. As an example, a photocopy or electronic copy of the Self-Contained Appraisal Report, Summary Appraisal Report or Restricted Use Appraisal Report actually issued by an appraiser for a real property Complete Appraisal or Limited Appraisal assignment satisfies the true copy requirement for that assignment.
>
> Care should be exercised in the selection of the form, style, and type of medium for written records, which may be handwritten and informal, to ensure they are retrievable by the appraiser throughout the prescribed record retention period.
>
> A workfile must be in existence prior to and contemporaneous with the issuance of a written or oral report. A written summary of an oral report must be added to the workfile within a reasonable time after the issuance of the oral report.
>
> A workfile must be made available by the appraiser when required by state enforcement agencies or due process of law. In addition, a workfile in support of a Restricted Use Appraisal Report must be available for inspection by the client in accordance with the Comment to Standards Rule 2-2(c)(ix), 8-2(c)(ix) and 10-2(b)(ix).

COMPETENCY RULE

Prior to accepting an assignment or entering into an agreement to perform any assignment, an appraiser must properly identify the problem to be addressed and have the knowledge and experience to complete the assignment competently; or alternatively:

1.   disclose the lack of knowledge and/or experience to the client before accepting the assignment; and
2.   take all steps necessary or appropriate to complete the assignment competently; and
3.   describe the lack of knowledge and/or experience and the steps taken to complete the assignment competently in the report.

>   Comment: Competency applies to factors such as, but not limited to, an appraiser's familiarity with a specific type of property, a market, a geographic area, or an analytical method. If such a factor is necessary for an appraiser to develop credible appraisal assignment results, the appraiser is responsible for having the competency to address that factor, or for following the steps outlined above to satisfy this Competency Rule.

>   The background and experience of appraisers varies widely and a lack of knowledge or experience can lead to inaccurate or inappropriate appraisal practice. The COMPETENCY RULE requires an appraiser to have both the knowledge and the experience required to perform a specific appraisal service competently.

>   If an appraiser is offered the opportunity to perform an appraisal service but lacks the necessary knowledge or experience to complete it competently, the appraiser must disclose his or her lack of knowledge or experience to the client before accepting the assignment and then take the necessary or appropriate steps to complete the appraisal service competently. This may be accomplished in various ways including, but not limited to, personal study by the appraiser; association with an appraiser reasonably believed to have the necessary knowledge or experience; or retention of others who possess the required knowledge or experience.

>   In an assignment where geographic competency is necessary, an appraiser preparing an appraisal in an unfamiliar location must spend sufficient time to understand the nuances of the local market and the supply and demand factors relating to the specific property type and the location involved. Such understanding will not be imparted solely from a consideration of specific data such as demographics, costs, sales, and rentals. The necessary understanding of local market conditions provides the bridge between a sale and a comparable sale or a rental and a comparable rental. If an appraiser is not in a position to spend the necessary amount of time in a market area to obtain this understanding, affiliation with a qualified local appraiser may be the appropriate response to ensure development of credible assignment results.

>   Although this rule requires an appraiser to identify the problem and disclose any deficiency in competence prior to accepting an assignment, facts or conditions uncovered during the course of an assignment could cause an appraiser to discover that he or she lacks the required knowledge or experience to complete the assignment competently. At the point of such discovery, the appraiser is obligated to notify the client and comply with items 2 and 3 of the rule.

DEPARTURE RULE

This rule permits limited exceptions to sections of the Uniform Standards that are classified as specific requirements rather than binding requirements. The burden of proof is on the appraiser to decide before accepting an assignment and invoking this rule that the scope of work applied will result in opinions or conclusions that are credible. The burden of disclosure is also on the appraiser to report any departures from specific requirements.

An appraiser may enter into an agreement to perform an assignment in which the scope of the work is less than, or different from, the work that would otherwise be required by the specific requirements , provided that prior to entering into such an agreement:

DEPARTURE RULE (continued)

1.   the appraiser has determined that the appraisal or consulting process to be performed is not so limited that the results of the assignment are no longer credible;
2.   the appraiser has advised the client that the assignment calls for something less than, or different from, the work required by the specific requirements and that the report will clearly identify and explain the departure(s); and
3.   the client has agreed that the performance of a limited appraisal or consulting service would be appropriate, given the intended use.

Comment: Not all specific requirements are *applicable* to every assignment. When a specific requirement is *not applicable* to a given assignment, the specific requirement is irrelevant and therefore no departure is needed.

A specific requirement is *applicable* when:
- it addresses factors or conditions that are present in the given assignment, or
- it addresses analysis that is typical practice in such an assignment.

A specific requirement is *not applicable* when:
- it addresses factors or conditions that are not present in the given assignment, or
- it addresses analysis that is not typical practice in such an assignment, or
- it addresses analysis that would not provide meaningful results in the given assignment.

Of these specific requirements that are *applicable* to a given assignment, some may be *necessary* in order to result in opinions or conclusions that are credible. When a specific requirement is necessary to a given assignment, departure is not permitted.

Departure is permitted from those specific requirements that are *applicable* to a given assignment, but *not necessary* in order to result in opinions or conclusions that are credible.

A specific requirement is considered to be *applicable* and *necessary* when:
- it addresses factors or conditions that are present in the given assignment, or
- it addresses analysis that is typical practice in such an assignment, and
- lack of consideration for those factors, conditions or analyses would significantly affect the credibility of the results.

Typical practice for a given assignment is measured by:
- the expectations of the participants in the market for appraisal services, and
- what an appraiser's peers' actions would be in performing the same or a similar assignment.

If an appraiser enters into an agreement to perform an appraisal or consulting service that calls for something less than, or different from, the work that would otherwise be required by the specific appraisal requirements, Standards Rules 2-2(a)(xi), 2-2(b)(xi), 2-2(c)(xi), 5-2(i), 8-2(a)(xi), 8-2(b)(xi), 8-2(c)(xi), 10-2(a)(x) and 10-2(b)(x) require that the report clearly identify and explain departure(s) from the specific requirements.

Departure from the following development and reporting rules is not permitted: Standards Rules 1-1, 1-2, 1-5, 2-1, 2-2, 2-3, 3-1, 3-2, 4-1, 5-1, 5-3, 6-1, 6-3, 6-6, 6-7, 6-8, 7-1, 7-2, 8-1, 8-2, 8-3, 8-4, 8-5, 9-1, 9-2, 9-3, and 9-5, 10-1, 10-2, 10-3, and 10-5. This restriction on departure is reiterated throughout the document with the reminder: "This Standards Rule contains binding requirements from which departure is not permitted."

The DEPARTURE RULE does not apply to the PREAMBLE, ETHICS RULE, COMPETENCY RULE, JURISDICTIONAL EXCEPTION, SUPPLEMENTAL STANDARDS, or DEFINITIONS Section.

JURISDICTIONAL EXCEPTION RULE

If any part of these standards is contrary to the law or public policy of any jurisdiction, only that part shall be void and of no force or effect in that jurisdiction.

> Comment: The purpose of the JURISDICTIONAL EXCEPTION RULE is strictly limited to providing a saving or severability clause intended to preserve the balance of USPAP if one or more of its parts are determined as contrary to law or public policy of a jurisdiction. By logical extension, there can be no violation of USPAP by an appraiser disregarding, with proper disclosure, only the part or parts of USPAP that are void and of no force and effect in a particular assignment by operation of legal authority. It is misleading for an appraiser to disregard a part or parts of USPAP as void and of no force and effect in a particular assignment without identifying the part or parts disregarded and the legal authority justifying this action in the appraiser's report.
>
> As used in the JURISDICTIONAL EXCEPTION RULE, law means a body of rules with binding legal force established by controlling governmental authority. This broad meaning includes, without limitation, the federal and state constitutions, legislative and court made law, and administrative rules, regulations, and ordinances. Public policy refers to more or less well defined moral and ethical standards of conduct, currently and generally accepted by the community as a whole, and recognized by the courts with the aid of statutes, judicial precedents, and other similar available evidence. Jurisdiction relates to the legal authority to legislate, apply, or interpret law in any form at the federal, state, and local levels of government.

SUPPLEMENTAL STANDARDS RULE

These Uniform Standards provide the common basis for all appraisal practice. Supplemental standards applicable to appraisals prepared for specific purposes or property types may be issued (i.e. published) by public agencies and other entities that establish public policy. An appraiser and client must ascertain whether any such published supplemental standards in addition to these Uniform Standards apply to the assignment being considered.

> Comment: The purpose of the Supplemental Standards Rule is to provide a reasonable means to augment USPAP with requirements that add to the requirements set forth by USPAP.
>
> Supplemental standards cannot diminish the purpose, intent, or content of the requirements of USPAP.
>
> Upon agreeing to perform an assignment that includes acceptable supplemental standards, an appraiser is obligated to competently satisfy those supplemental standards, as well as applicable USPAP requirements.
>
> An appraiser who represents that an assignment is or will be completed in compliance with agreed-upon supplemental standards and who then knowingly fails to comply with those supplemental standards violates the ETHICS RULE, or who then immediately fails to comply with those supplemental standards violates the COMPETENCY RULE. (See the ETHICS RULE and the COMPETENCY RULE.)

DEFINITIONS

For the purpose of these standards, the following definitions apply:

ADVOCACY: representing the cause or interest of another, even if that cause or interest does not necessarily conincide with one's own beliefs, opinions, conclusions, or recommendations.

DEFINITIONS (continued)

APPRAISAL: **(noun) the act or process of developing an opinion of value; an opinion of value;**
          (adjective) of or pertaining to appraising and related functions, e.g. appraisal practice, appraisal services.

> **Complete Appraisal:** **the act of developing an opinion of value or an opinion of value developed without invoking the DEPARTURE RULE.**

> **Limited Appraisal:** **the act or process of developing an opinion of value or an opinion of value developed under and resulting from invoking the DEPARTURE RULE.**

> Comment: An opinion of value must be numerically expressed as a specific amount, as a range of numbers, or as a relationship (e.g., not more than, not less than) to a previous value opinion or numerical benchmark (e.g., assessed value, collateral value).

APPRAISAL CONSULTING: the act or process of developing an analysis, recommendation or opinion to solve a problem where an opinion of value is a component of the analysis leading to the assignment results.

> Comment: An appraisal consulting assignment involves an opinion of value but does not have an appraisal or an appraisal review as its primary purpose

APPRAISAL PRACTICE: valuation services, including but not limited to appraisal, appraisal review, or appraisal consulting, performed by an individual as an appraiser.

> Comment: Appraisal practice is provided only by appraisers while valuation services are provided by a variety of professionals and others. The terms *appraisal, appraisal review*, and *appraisal consulting* are intentionally generic and are not mutually exclusive. For example, an opinion of value may be required as part of an appraisal review and is required as a component of the analysis in an appraisal consulting assignment. The use of other nomenclature for an appraisal, appraisal review or appraisal consulting assignment (e.g., analysis, counseling, evaluation study, submission, valuation) does not exempt an appraiser from adherence to the *Uniform Standards of Professional Appraisal Practice.*

APPRAISAL REVIEW: the act or process of developing and communicating an opinion about the quality of another appraiser's work.

> Comment: The subject of an appraisal review assignment may be all or part of an appraisal report, the work file, or a combination of these.

APPRAISER: one who is expected to perform valuation services competently and in a manner that is independent, impartial and objective.

> Comment: Such expectation occurs when individuals, either by choice or by requirement placed upon them or upon the service they provide by law, regulation, or agreement with the client or intended users, represent that they comply (See PREAMBLE.)

APPRAISER'S PEERS: other appraisers who have expertise and competency in the same or similar type of assignment.

ASSIGNMENT: a valuation service provided as a consequence of an agreement between an appraiser and client.

DEFINITIONS (continued)

ASSIGNMENT RESULTS: an appraiser's opinions and conclusions developed specific to an assignment.

> Comment: Assignment results are an appraiser's:
> - opinions or conclusions developed in an appraisal assignment, such as value;
> - opinions of adequacy, relevancy or reasonableness developed in an appraisal review assignment; or
> - opinions, conclusions or recommendations developed in an appraisal consulting assignment.

ASSUMPTION: that which is taken to be true.

BIAS: a preference or inclination used in the development or communication of an appraisal, appraisal review, or consulting assignment that precludes an appraiser's impartiality.

BINDING REQUIREMENT: all or part of a standards rule of a Standards Rule of USPAP from which departure is not permitted. (See Departure Rule)

BUSINESS ENTERPRISE: an entity pursuing an economic activity.

BUSINESS EQUITY: the interests, benefits, and rights inherent in the ownership of a business enterprise or a part thereof in any form (including but not necessarily limited to capital stock, partnership interests, cooperatives, sole proprietorships, options, and warrants).

CASH FLOW ANALYSIS: a study of the anticipated movement of cash into or out of an investment.

CLIENT: the party or parties who engages an appraiser (by employment or contract) in a specific assignment.

> Comment: The client identified by the appraiser in an appraisal, consulting, or review report (or in the assignment workfile) is the party or parties with whom the appraiser has an appraiser-client relationship in the related assignment and may be an individual, group, or entity.

CONFIDENTIAL INFORMATION: information that is either:
- identified by the client as confidential when providing it to an appraiser and that is not available from any other source; or
- classified as confidential or private by applicable law or regulation

COST: the amount required to create, produce or obtain a property.

> Comment: Cost is either a fact or an estimate of fact.

EXTRAORDINARY ASSUMPTION: an assumption, directly related to a specific assignment, which, if found to be false, could alter the appraiser's opinions or conclusions.

> Comment: Extraordinary assumptions presume as fact otherwise uncertain information about physical, legal or economic characteristics of the subject property or about conditions external to the property (such as market conditions or trends, or the integrity of data used in an analysis).

FEASIBILITY ANALYSIS: a study of the cost-benefit relationship of an economic endeavor.

DEFINITIONS (continued)

HYPOTHETICAL CONDITION: that which is contrary to what exists, but is supposed for the purpose of analysis.

> Comment: Hypothetical conditions assume conditions contrary to known facts about physical, legal or economic characteristics of the subject property or about conditions external to the property (such as market conditions or trends, or the integrity of data used in an analysis).

INTANGIBLE PROPERTY (INTANGIBLE ASSETS): non-physical assets, including but not limited to franchises, trademarks, patents, copyrights, goodwill, equities, mineral rights, securities, and contracts, as distinguished from physical assets such as facilities and equipment.

INTENDED USE: the use or uses of an appraiser's reported appraisal, consulting, or review assignment opinions and conclusions, as identified by the appraiser based on communication with the client at the time of the assignment.

INTENDED USER: the client and any other party as identified, by name or type, as users of the appraisal, consulting, or review report, by the appraiser based on communication with the client at the time of the assignment.

INVESTMENT ANALYSIS: a study that reflects the relationship between acquisition price and anticipated future benefits of a real estate investment.

JURISDICTIONAL EXCEPTION: an assignment condition that voids the force of a part or parts of USPAP, when compliance with part or parts of USPAP is contrary to law or public policy applicable to the assignment.

MARKET ANALYSIS: a study of real estate market conditions for a specific type of property.

MARKET VALUE: a type of value, stated as an opinion, that presumes the transfer of a property (i.e., a right of ownership or a bundle of such rights), as of a certain date, under specific conditions set forth in the definition of the term identified by the appraiser as applicable in an appraisal.

> Comment: Forming an opinion of market value is the purpose of many real property appraisal assignments, particularly when the client's intended use includes more than one intended user. The conditions included in market value definitions establish market perspectives for development of the opinion. These conditions may vary from definition to definition, but generally fall into three categories:
> 1. the relationship, knowledge, and motivation of the parties (i.e., seller and buyer)
> 2. the terms of sale (e.g., cash, cash equivalent, or other terms); and
> 3. the conditions of sale (e.g., exposure in a competitive market for a reasonable time prior to sale).
>
> *Appraisers are cautioned to identify the exact definition of market value, and its authority, applicable in each appraisal completed for the purpose of market value.*

MASS APPRAISAL: the process of valuing a universe of properties as of a given date utilizing standard methodology, employing common data, and allowing for statistical testing.

MASS APPRAISAL MODEL: a mathematical expression of how supply and demand factors interact in a market.

PERSONAL PROPERTY: identifiable portable and tangible objects which are considered by the general public as being "personal," e.g. furnishings, artwork, antiques, gems and jewelry, collectibles, machinery and equipment; all tangible property that is not classified as real estate.

DEFINITIONS (continued)

PRICE: the amount asked, offered, or paid for a property.

> Comment: Once stated, *price* is a fact, whether it is publicly disclosed or retained in private. Because of the financial capabilities, motivations, or special interests of a given buyer or seller, the price paid for a property may or may not have any relation to the *value* which might be ascribed to that property by others.

REAL ESTATE: an identified parcel or tract of land, including improvements, if any.

REAL PROPERTY: the interests, benefits, and rights inherent in the ownership of real estate.

> Comment: In some jurisdictions, the terms real estate and real property have the same legal meaning. The separate definitions recognize the traditional distinction between the two concepts in appraisal theory.

REPORT: any communication, written or oral, of an appraisal, appraisal review, or consulting service that is transmitted to the client upon completion of an assignment.

> Comment: Most reports are written and most clients mandate written reports. Oral report requirements (See the Record Keeping section of the ETHICS RULE) are included to cover court testimony and other oral communications of an appraisal, appraisal review or consulting service.
>
> The types of written reports listed below apply to real property, personal property and business valuation assignments, as indicated
> **Appraisal Report: a written report prepared under Standards Rule 10-2(a).**
> **Self-Contained Appraisal Report: a written report prepared under Standards Rule 2-2(a) or 8-2(a).**
> **Summary Appraisal Report: a written report prepared under Standards Rule 2-2(b) or 8-2(b).**
> **Restricted Use Appraisal Report: a written report prepared under Standards Rule 2-2(c), 8-2(c) or 10-2(b).**

SCOPE OF WORK: the amount and type of information researched and the analysis applied in an assignment. Scope of work includes, but it not limited to, the following:
- **the degree to which the property is inspected or identified;**
- **the extent of research into physical or economic factors that could affect the property**
- **the extent of data research; and**
- **the type and extent of analysis applied to arrive at opinions or conclusions.**

SIGNATURE: personalized evidence indicating authentication of the work performed by the appraiser and the acceptance of the responsibility for content, analyses, and the conclusions in the report.

> Comment: A signature can be represented by a handwritten mark, a digitized image controlled by a personalized identification number, or other media, where the appraiser has sole personalized control of affixing the signature.

SPECIFIC REQUIREMENT: all or part of a Standards Rule of USPAP from which departure is permitted under certain limited conditions. (See DEPARTURE RULE)

SUPPLEMENTAL STANDARDS: requirements issued by government agencies or other entities that establish public policy which add to the purpose, intent and content of the requirements in USPAP, that have a material effect on the development and reporting of assignment results.

> Comment: Supplemental standards are published in regulations, rules, policies and other similar documents, and have the same applicability to all properties or assignments in a particular category or class regardless of the contracting entity.

DEFINITIONS (continued)

Supplemental standards are different from other contractual agreements that are unique to the contracting entity and which apply specifically to a particular property or assignment.

VALUE: the monetary relationship between properties and those who buy, sell or use those properties.

Comment: *Value* expresses an economic concept. As such, it is never a fact, but always an opinion of the worth of a property at a given time in accordance with a specific definition of value. In appraisal practice, value must always be qualified, e.g., market value, liquidation value, investment value.

VALUE SERVICES: services pertaining to aspects of property value.

Comment: Valuation services pertain to all aspects of property value and include services performed both by appraisers and by others.

WORKFILE: documentation necessary to support an appraiser's analysis, opinions and conclusions.

STANDARD 1 REAL PROPERTY APPRAISAL, DEVELOPMENT

In developing a real property appraisal, an appraiser must identify the problem to be solved and the scope of work necessary to solve the problem, and correctly complete research and analysis necessary to produce a credible appraisal.

Comment: STANDARD 1 is directed toward the substantive aspects of developing a competent appraisal of real property. The requirement set forth in STANDARD 1 follow the appraisal development process in the order of topics addressed and can be used by appraisers and the users of appraisal services as a convenient checklist.

Standards Rule 1-1 (This Standard Rule contains binding requirements from which departure is not permitted.)

In developing a real property appraisal, an appraiser must:

(a)   be aware of, understand, and correctly employ those recognized methods and techniques that are necessary to produce a credible appraisal;

Comment: This rule recognizes that the principle of change continues to affect the manner in which appraisers perform appraisal services. Changes and developments in the real estate field have a substantial impact on the appraisal profession. Important changes in the cost and manner of constructing and marketing commercial, industrial, and residential real estate as well as changes in the legal framework in which real property rights and interests are created, conveyed, and mortgaged have resulted in corresponding changes in appraisal theory and practice. Social change has also had an effect on appraisal theory and practice. To keep abreast of these changes and developments, the appraisal profession is constantly reviewing and revising appraisal methods and techniques and devising new methods and techniques to meet new circumstances. For this reason it is not sufficient for appraisers to simply maintain the skills and the knowledge they possess when they become appraisers. Each appraiser must continuously improve his or her skills to remain proficient in real property appraisal.

(b)   not commit a substantial error of omission or commission that significantly affects an appraisal;

Comment: In performing appraisal services, an appraiser must be certain that the gathering of factual information is conducted in a manner that is sufficiently diligent, given the scope of work as identified according to Standard 1-2(f), to ensure that the data that would have a material or significant effect on the resulting opinions or conclusions are identified and, where necessary, analyzed. Further, an appraiser must use sufficient care in analyzing such data to avoid errors that would significantly affect his or her opinions and conclusions.

STANDARD 1 (continued)

(c)   **not render appraisal services in a careless or negligent manner, such as by making a series of errors that, although individually might not significantly affect the results of an appraisal, in the aggregate affect the credibility of those results.**

Comment: Perfection is impossible to attain and competence does not require perfection. However, an appraiser must not render appraisal services in a careless or negligent manner. This rule requires an appraiser to use due diligence and due care. The fact that the carelessness or negligence of an appraiser has not caused an error that significantly affects his or her opinions or conclusions and thereby seriously harms an intended user does not excuse such carelessness or negligence.

Standards Rule 1-2 (This Standard Rule contains binding requirements from which **departure is not permitted.**

In developing a real property appraisal, an appraiser must:

(a)   **identify the client and other intended users;**

(b)   **identify the intended use of the appraiser's opinions and conclusions;**

Comment: Identification of the intended use is necessary for the appraiser and the client to decide:
● the appropriate scope of work to be completed, and
● the level of information to be provided in communicating the appraisal.

An appraiser must not allow a client's objectives or intended use to cause an analysis to be biased.

(c)   **identify the purpose of the assignment, including the type and definition of value to be developed; and, if the value opinion to be developed is market value, ascertain whether the value is to be the most probable price:**

   (i)   in terms of cash; or
   (ii)   in terms of financial arrangements equivalent to cash; or
   (iii) in other precisely defined terms; and
   (iv) if the opinion of value is to be based on non-market financing or financing with unusual conditions or incentives, the terms of such financing must be clearly identified and the appraiser's opinion of their contributions to or negative influence on value must be developed by analysis of relevant market data.

Comment: When the purpose of an assignment is to develop an opinion of market value, the appraiser must also develop an opinion of reasonable exposure time linked to the value opinion.

(d)   **identify the effective date of the appraiser's opinions and conclusions;**

(e)   **identify the characteristics of the property that are relevant to the purpose and intended use of the appraisal, including:**

   (i)   its location and physical, legal, and economic attributes;
   (ii)   the real property interest to be valued;
   (iii) any personal property, trade fixtures or intangible items that are not real property but are included in the appraisal;
   (iv) any known easements, restrictions, encumbrances, leases, reservations, covenants, contracts, declarations, special assessments, ordinances, or other items of a similar nature;
   (v)   whether the subject property is a fractional interest, physical segment, or partial holding.

STANDARD 1 (continued)

Comment on (i) - (v): If the necessary subject property information is not available due to assignment conditions that limit research opportunity (such as conditions that preclude an on-site inspection or the gathering of information from reliable third-party sources), an appraiser must:
- obtain the necessary information before proceeding, or
- where possible, in compliance with Standards Rule 1-2(g), use an extraordinary assumption about such information.

An appraiser may use any combination of a property inspection and documents, such as a physical legal description, address, map reference, copy of a survey or map, property sketch, or photographs, to identify the relevant characteristics of the subject property. Identification of the real property interest appraised can be based on a review of copies or summaries of title descriptions or other documents that set forth any known encumbrances. The information used by an appraiser to identify the property characteristics must be from sources the appraiser reasonably believes are reliable. An appraiser is not required to value the whole when the subject of the appraisal is a fractional interest, a physical segment, or a partial holding

(f)   **identify the scope of work necessary to complete the assignment;**

Comment: The scope of work is acceptable when it is consistent with:
- the expectations of participants in the market for the same or similar appraisal services, and
- what the appraiser's peers' actions would be in performing the same or similar assignment in compliance with USPAP.

An appraiser must have sound reasons in support of the scope of work decisions, and be prepared to support the decision to exclude any information or procedure that would appear to be relevant to the client, an intended user, or the appraiser's peers in the same or similar assignment.

An appraiser must not allow assignment conditions or other factors to limit the extent of research or analysis to such a degree that the resulting opinions and conclusions developed in an assignment are not credible in the context of the intended use of the appraisal.

(g)   **identify any extraordinary assumptions necessary in the assignment;**

Comment: An extraordinary assumption may be used in an assignment only if:
- it is required to properly develop credible opinions and conclusions;
- the appraiser has a reasonable basis for the extraordinary assumption;
- use of the extraordinary assumption results in a credible analysis; and
- the appraiser complies with the disclosure requirements set forth in USPAP for extraordinary assumptions

(h)   **identify any hypothetical conditions necessary in the assignment.**

Comment: A hypothetical condition may be used in an assignment only if:
- use of the hypothetical condition is clearly required for legal purposes, for purposes of reasonable analysis, or for purposes of comparison;
- use of the hypothetical condition results in a credible analysis; and
- the appraiser complies with the disclosure requirements set forth in USPAP for hypothetical conditions.

Standards Rule 1-3 (This Standards Rule contains specific requirements from which departure is permitted. See the DEPARTURE RULE.)

When the value opinion to be developed is market value, and given the scope of work identified in accordance with Standards Rule 1-2(f), an appraiser must:

STANDARD 1 (continued)

(a)   **identify and analyze the effect on use and value of existing land use regulations, reasonably probable modifications of such land use regulations, economic demand, the physical adaptability of the real estate, and market area trends;**

Comment: An appraiser must avoid making an unsupported assumption or premise about market area trends, effective age, and remaining life.

(b)   **develop an opinion of the highest and best use of the real estate.**

Comment: An appraiser must analyze the relevant legal, physical, and economic factors to the extent necessary to support the appraiser's highest and best use conclusion(s). The appraiser must recognize that land is appraised as though vacant and available for development to its highest and best use, and that the appraisal of improvements is based on their actual contribution to the site.

Standards Rule 1-4 **(This Standards Rule contains specific requirements from which departure is permitted. See the DEPARTURE RULE.)**

In developing a real property appraisal, an appraiser must collect, verify, and analyze all information pertinent to the appraisal problem, given the scope of work identified in accordance with Standards Rule 1-2(f).

(a)   **When a sales comparison approach is applicable, an appraiser must analyze such comparable sales data, as are available to indicate a value conclusion.**

(b)   **When a cost approach approach is applicable, an appraiser must:**
    (i)   **develop an opinion of site value by an appropriate appraisal method or technique ;**
    (ii)   **analyze such comparable cost data as are available to estimate the cost new of the improvements(if any);**
    (iii)   **analyze such comparable data as are available to estimate the difference between cost new and the present worth of the improvements (accrued depreciation).**

(c)   **When an income approach to value is applicable, an appraiser must:**
    (i)   **analyze such comparable rental data as are available to estimate the market rental of the property;**
    (ii)   **analyze such comparable operating expense data as are available to estimate the operating expenses of the property;**
    (iii)   **analyze such comparable data as are available to estimate rates of capitalization and/or rates of discount; and**
    (iv)   **base projections of future rent and expenses on reasonably clear and appropriate evidence.**

Comment: An appraiser must, in developing income and expense statements and cash flow projections, weigh historical information and trends, current supply and demand factors affecting such trends, and anticipated events such as competition from developments under construction.

(d)   **When developing an opinion of the value of a leased fee estate or a leasehold estate, an appraiser must analyze the effect on value, if any, of the terms and conditions of the lease(s).**

(e)   **An appraiser must analyze the effect on value, if any, of the assemblage of the various estates or component parts of a property and refrain from valuing the whole solely by adding together the individual values of the various estates or component parts.**

STANDARD 1 (continued)

Comment: Although the value of the whole may be equal to the sum of the separate estates or parts, it also may be greater than or less that the sum of such estates or parts. Therefore, the value of the whole must be tested by reference to appropriate data and supported by an appropriate analysis of such data.

A similar procedure must be followed when the value of the whole has been established and the appraiser seeks to value a part. The value of any such part must be tested by reference to appropriate data and supported by an appropriate analysis of such data.

(f) **An appraiser must analyze the effect on value, if any, of anticipated public or private improvements, located on or off the site, to the extent that market actions reflect such anticipated improvements as of the effective appraisal date.**

(g) **An appraiser must analyze the effect on value of any personal property, trade fixtures or intangible items that are not real property but are included in the appraisal.**

Comment: Competency in personal property appraisal (See STANDARD 7) or business valuation (See STANDARD 9) may be required when it is necessary to allocate the overall value to the property components. A separate valuation, developed in compliance with the Standard pertinent to the type of property involved, is required when the value of a non-realty item or combination of such items is significant to the overall value.

(h) **When appraising proposed improvements, an appraiser must examine and have available for future examination:**

(i) **plans, specifications, or other documentation sufficient to identify the scope and character of the proposed improvements;**
(ii) **evidence indicating the probable time of completion of the proposed improvements; and**
(iii) **reasonably clear and appropriate evidence supporting development costs, anticipated earnings, occupancy projections, and the anticipated competition at the time of completion.**

Comment: Development of a value opinion for a subject property with proposed improvements as of a current date involves the use of the hypothetical condition that the described improvements have been completed as of the date of value when, in fact, they have not.

The evidence required to be examined and maintained may include such items as contractor's estimates relating to cost and the time required to complete construction, market, and feasibility studies; operating cost data; and the history of recently completed similar developments. The appraisal may require a complete feasibility analysis (See Standards Rule 4-6).

Standards Rule 1-5 (This Standard Rule contains binding requirements from which departure is not permitted.)

In developing a real property appraisal, an appraiser must:

(a) **analyze any current Agreement of Sale, option, or listing of the property, if such information is available to the appraiser in the normal course of business;**

(b) **analyze any prior sales of the property that occurred within the following minimum time periods:**

(i) **one year for one-to-four family residential property; and**
(ii) **three years for all other property types;**

STANDARD 1 (continued)

(c)   **reconcile the quality and quantity of data available and analyzed within the approaches used and the applicability or suitability of the approaches used.**

Comment: See the Comments to Standards Rules 2-2(a)(ix), 2-2(b)(ix), and 2-2(c)(ix) for corresponding reporting requirements.

STANDARD 2 REAL PROPERTY APPRAISAL REPORTING

In reporting the results of a real property appraisal an appraiser must communicate each analysis, opinion, and conclusion in a manner that is not misleading.

Comment: STANDARD 2 addresses the content and level of information required in a report that communicates the results of a real property appraisal.

STANDARD 2 does not dictate the from, format, or style of real property appraisal reports. The form, format and style of a report are functions of the needs of users and appraisers. The substantive content of a report determines its compliance.

Standards Rule 2-1 (This Standards Rule contains binding requirements from which departure is not permitted.)

Each written or oral real property appraisal report must:

(a)   **clearly and accurately set forth the appraisal in a manner that will not be misleading;**

(b)   **contain sufficient information to enable the intended users of the appraisal to understand the report properly;**

(c)   **clearly and accurately disclose any extraordinary assumption, hypothetical condition, or limiting condition that directly affects the appraisal and indicate its impact on value.**

Comment: Examples of extraordinary assumptions or hypothetical conditions might include items such as the execution of a pending lease agreement, atypical financing, a known but not yet quantified environmental issue, or completion of onsite or offsite improvements. In a written report the disclosure is required in conjunction with statements of each opinion or conclusion that is affected.

Standards Rule 2-2 (This Standard Rule contains binding requirements from which departure is not permitted.)

Each written real property appraisal report must be prepared under one of the following three options and prominently state which option is used: Self-Contained Appraisal Report, Summary Appraisal Report or Restricted Use Appraisal Report.

Comment: When the intended users include parties other than the client, either a Self-Contained Appraisal Report or a Summary Appraisal Report must be provided. When the intended users do not include parties other than the client, a Restricted Use Appraisal Report may be provided.

The essential difference among the three options is in the content and level of information provided.

STANDARD 2 (continued)

An appraiser must use care when characterizing the type of report and level of information communicated upon completion of an assignment. An appraiser may use any other label in addition to, but not in place of, the label set forth in this Standard for the type of report provided.

The report content and level of information requirements set forth in this Standard are minimums for each type of report. An appraiser mus supplement a report form, when necessary, to ensure any intended user of the appraisal is not misled and the report complies with the applicable content requirements set forth in this Standards Rule.

A party receiving a copy of a Self-Contained Appraisal Report, Summary Appraisal Report or a Restricted Use Appraisal Report in order to satisfy disclosure requirements does not become an intended user of the appraisal unless the client identifies such party as an intended user as part of the assignment.

(a)   **The content of a Self-Contained Appraisal Report must be consistent with the intended use of the appraisal and, at a minimum:**

   (i)   **state the identity of the client and any intended users, by name or type;**

   Comment: An appraiser must use care when identifying the client to ensure a clear understanding and to avoid violations of the Confidentiality Section of the ETHICS RULE. In those rare instances where the client wishes to remain anonymous, an appraiser must still document the identity of the client in the workfile, but may omit the client's identity in the report.

   Intended users of the report might include parties such as lenders, employees of government agencies, partners of a client, and a client's attorney and accountant.

   (ii)   **state the intended use of the appraisal;**

   (iii)   **describe information sufficient to identify the real estate involved in the appraisal, including the physical and economic property characteristics relevant to the assignment;**

   Comment: The real estate involved in the appraisal can be specified, for example, by a legal description, address, map reference, copy of a survey or map, property sketch and/or photographs or the like. The information can include a property sketch and photographs in addition to written comments about the legal, physical and economic attributes of the real estate relevant to the purpose and intended use of the appraisal.

   (iv)   **state the real property interest appraised;**

   Comment : The statement of the real property rights being appraised must be substantiated, as needed, by copies or summaries of title descriptions or other documents that set forth any known encumbrances.

   (v)   **state the purpose of the appraisal, including the type and definition of value and its source;**

   Comment: Stating the definition of value requires the definition itself, an appropriate reference to the source of the definition, and any comments needed to clearly indicate to the reader how the definition is being applied.

   When the purpose of the assignment is to develop an opinion of market value, state whether the opinion of value is:
   - in terms of cash or on financing terms equivalent to cash, or
   - based on sub-market financing or financing with unusual conditions or incentives; and,

STANDARD 2 (continued)

- when the opinion of value is not in terms of cash or based on financing terms equivalent to cash, summarize the terms of such financing and explain their contributions to or negative influence on value.

(vi)   state the effective date of the appraisal and the date of the report;

Comment: The effective date of the appraisal establishes the context for the value opinion, while the date of the report indicates whether the perspective of the appraiser on the market or property use conditions as of the effective date of the appraisal was prospective, current, or retrospective.

Reiteration of the date of the report and the effective date of the appraisal at various stages of the report in tandem is important for the clear understanding of the reader whenever market or property use conditions on the date of the report are different from such conditions on the effective date of the appraisal.

(vii)   describe sufficient information to disclose to the client and any intended users of the appraisal the scope of work used to develop the appraisal;

Comment: This requirement is to ensure that the client and intended users whose expected reliance on an appraisal may be affected by the extent of the appraiser's investigation are properly informed and are not misled as to the scope of work. The appraiser has the burden of proof to support the scope of work decision and the level of information included in a report.

When any portion of the work involves significant real property appraisal assistance, the appraiser must describe the extent of that assistance. The signing appraiser must also state the name(s) of those providing the significant real property appraisal assistance in the certification, in accordance with SR 2-3.

(viii) set forth all assumptions, hypothetical conditions and limiting conditions that affected the analyses, opinions, and conclusions;

Comment: Typical or ordinary assumptions and limiting conditions may be grouped together in an identified section of the report. An extraordinary assumption or hypothetical condition must be disclosed in conjunction with statements of each opinion or conclusion that is affected.

(ix)   describe the information analyzed, the appraisal procedures followed, and the reasoning that supports the analyses, opinions, and conclusions;

Comment: The appraiser must be certain the sufficient information is sufficient for the client and intended users to adequately understand the rationale for the opinion and conclusions.

When the purpose of an assignment is to develop an opinion of market value, a summary of the results of analyzing the information required in Standards Rule 1-5 is required. If such information was unobtainable, a statement on the efforts undertaken by the appraiser to obtain the information is required. If such information is irrelevant, a statement acknowledging the existence of the information and citing its lack of relevance is required.

(x)   state the use of the real estate, existing as of the date of value, and the use of the real estate reflected in the appraisal; and, when the purpose of the assignment is market value, describe the support and rationale for the appraiser's opinion of the highest and best use of the real estate;

STANDARD 2 (continued)

> <u>Comment</u>: The report must contain the appraiser's opinion as to the highest and best use of the real estate, unless an opinion as to highest and best use is unnecessary, e.g. insurance valuation or "value in use" appraisals. If the purpose of the assignment is market value, the appraiser's support and rationale for the opinion of highest and best use is required. The appraiser's reasoning in support of the opinion must be provided in the depth and detail required by its significance to the appraisal.

> (xi) **state and explain any permitted departures from specific requirements of STANDARD 1, and the reason for excluding any of the usual valuation approaches;**

> <u>Comment</u>: A Self-Contained Appraisal Report must include sufficient information to indicate that the appraiser complied with the requirements of STANDARD 1, including any permitted departures from the specific requirements. The amount of detail required will vary with the significance of the information to the appraisal.

> When the DEPARTURE RULE is invoked, the assignment is deemed to be a Limited Appraisal. Use of the term Limited Appraisal makes it clear that the assignment involved something less than, or different from the work required that could have and would have been completed if departure had not been invoked. The report of a Limited Appraisal must contain a prominent section that clearly identities the extent of the appraisal process performed and the departures taken.

> The reliability of the results of a Complete Appraisal or Limited Appraisal developed under STANDARD 1 is not affected by the type of report prepared under STANDARD 2. The extent of the appraisal process performed under STANDARD 1 is the basis for the reliability of the value conclusion.

> (xii) **include a signed certification in accordance with Standards Rule 2-3.**

(b) **The content of a Summary Appraisal Report must be consistent with the intended use of the appraisal and, at a minimum:**

> <u>Comment</u>: The essential difference between the Self-Contained Appraisal Report and the Summary Appraisal Report is the level of detail of presentation.

> (i) **state the identity of the client and any intended users, by name or type;**

> <u>Comment</u>: An appraiser must use care when identifying the client to ensure a clear understanding and to avoid violations of the Confidentiality Section of the ETHICS RULE. In those rare instances where the client wishes to remain anonymous, an appraiser must still document the identity of the client in the workfile, but may omit the client's identity in the report.

> Intended users of the report might include parties such as lenders, employees of government agencies, partners of a client, and a client's attorney and accountant.

> (ii) **state the intended use of the appraisal;**

> (iii) **summarize information sufficient to identify the real estate involved in the appraisal, including the physical and economic property characteristics relevant to the assignment;**

> <u>Comment</u>: The real estate involved in the appraisal can be specified, for example, by a legal description, address, map reference, copy of a survey or map, property sketch and/or photographs or the like. The summarized information can include a property sketch and photographs in addition to written comments

STANDARD 2 (continued)

about the legal, physical and economic attributes of the real estate relevant to the purpose and intended use of the appraisal.

(iv)   state the real property interest appraised;

Comment : The statement of the real property rights being appraised must be substantiated, as needed, by copies or summaries of title descriptions or other documents that set forth any known encumbrances.

(v)   state the purpose of the appraisal, including the type and definition of value and its source;

Comment: Stating the definition of value requires the definition itself, an appropriate reference to the source of the definition, and any comments needed to clearly indicate to the reader how the definition is being applied.

When the purpose of the assignment is to develop an opinion of market value, state whether the opinion of value is:
- in terms of cash or on financing terms equivalent to cash, or
- based on sub-market financing or financing with unusual conditions or incentives; and,
- when the opinion of value is not in terms of cash or based on financing terms equivalent to cash, summarize the terms of such financing and explain their contributions to or negative influence on value.

(vi)   state the effective date of the appraisal and the date of the report;

Comment: The effective date of the appraisal establishes the context for the value opinion, while the date of the report indicates whether the perspective of the appraiser on the market or property use conditions as of the effective date of the appraisal was prospective, current, or retrospective.

Reiteration of the date of the report and the effective date of the appraisal at various stages of the report in tandem is important for the clear understanding of the reader whenever market or property use conditions on the date of the report are different from such conditions on the effective date of the appraisal.

(vii)   summarize sufficient information to disclose to the client and any intended users of the appraisal the scope of work used to develop the appraisal;

Comment: This requirement is to ensure that the client and intended users whose expected reliance on an appraisal may be affected by the extent of the appraiser's investigation are properly informed and are not misled as to the scope of work. The appraiser has the burden of proof to support the scope of work decision and the level of information included in a report.

When any portion of the work involves significant real property appraisal assistance, the appraiser must summarize the extent of that assistance. The signing appraiser must also state the name(s) of those providing the significant real property appraisal assistance in the certification, in accordance with SR 2-3.

(viii)   state all assumptions, hypothetical conditions and limiting conditions that affected the analyses, opinions, and conclusions;

Comment: Typical or ordinary assumptions and limiting conditions may be grouped together in an identified section of the report. An extraordinary assumption or hypothetical condition must be disclosed in conjunction with statements of each opinion or conclusion that is affected.

STANDARD 2 (continued)

(ix) **summarize the information analyzed, the appraisal procedures followed, and the reasoning that supports the analyses, opinions, and conclusions;**

Comment: The appraiser must be certain the sufficient information is sufficient for the client and intended users to adequately understand the rationale for the opinion and conclusions.

When the purpose of an assignment is to develop an opinion of market value, a summary of the results of analyzing the information required in Standards Rule 1-5 is required. If such information was unobtainable, a statement on the efforts undertaken by the appraiser to obtain the information is required. If such information is irrelevant, a statement acknowledging the existence of the information and citing its lack of relevance is required.

(x) **state the use of the real estate, existing as of the date of value, and the use of the real estate reflected in the appraisal; and, when the purpose of the assignment is market value, summarize the support and rationale for the appraiser's opinion of the highest and best use of the real estate;**

Comment: The report must contain the appraiser's opinion as to the highest and best use of the real estate, unless an opinion as to highest and best use is unnecessary, e.g. insurance valuation or "value in use" appraisals. If the purpose of the assignment is market value, a summary of the appraiser's support and rationale for the opinion of highest and best use is required. The appraiser's reasoning in support of the opinion must be provided in the depth and detail required by its significance to the appraisal.

(xi) **state and explain any permitted departures from specific requirements of STANDARD 1, and the reason for excluding any of the usual valuation approaches;**

Comment: A Summary Appraisal Report must include sufficient information to indicate that the appraiser complied with the requirements of STANDARD 1, including any permitted departures from the specific requirements. The amount of detail required will vary with the significance of the information to the appraisal.

When the DEPARTURE RULE is invoked, the assignment is deemed to be a Limited Appraisal. Use of the term Limited Appraisal makes it clear that the assignment involved something less than, or different from the work required that could have and would have been completed if departure had not been invoked. The report of a Limited Appraisal must contain a prominent section that clearly identities the extent of the appraisal process performed and the departures taken.

The reliability of the results of a Complete Appraisal or Limited Appraisal developed under STANDARD 1 is not affected by the type of report prepared under STANDARD 2. The extent of the appraisal process performed under STANDARD 1 is the basis for the reliability of the value conclusion.

(xii) **include a signed certification in accordance with Standards Rule 2-3.**

(c) **The content of a Restricted Use Appraisal Report must be consistent with the intended use of the appraisal and, at a minimum:**

(i) **state the identity of the client and by name or type;**

Comment: An appraiser must use care when identifying the client to ensure a clear understanding and to avoid violations of the Confidentiality Section of the ETHICS RULE. In those rare instances where the

STANDARD 2 (continued)

client wishes to remain anonymous, an appraiser must still document the identity of the client in the workfile, but may omit the client's identity in the report. Intended users of the report might include parties such as lenders, employees of government agencies, partners of a client, and a client's attorney and accountant.

(ii)   **state the intended use of the appraisal;**

(iii)   **state information sufficient to identify the real estate involved in the appraisal;**

Comment: The real estate involved in the appraisal can be specified, for example, by a legal description, address, map reference, copy of a survey or map, property sketch and/or photographs.

(iv)   **state the real property interest appraised;**

(v)   **state the purpose of the appraisal, including the type and refer to the definition of value pertinent to the purpose of the assignment;**

(vi)   **state the effective date of the appraisal and the date of the report;**

Comment: The effective date of the appraisal establishes the context for the value opinion, while the date of the report indicates whether the perspective of the appraiser on the market or property use conditions as of the effective date of the appraisal was prospective, current, or retrospective.

(vii)   **state the extent of the process of collecting, confirming, and reporting data or refer to an assignment agreement retained in the appraiser's workfile, which describes the scope of work to be performed;**

Comment: When any portion of the work involves significant real property appraisal assistance, the appraiser must state the extent of that assistance. The signing appraiser must also state the name(s) of those providing the significant real property appraisal assistance in the certification, in accordance with SR 2-3.

(viii)   **state all assumptions, hypothetical conditions and limiting conditions that affect the analyses, opinions, and conclusions;**

Comment: Typical or ordinary assumptions and limiting conditions may be grouped together in an identified section of the report. An extraordinary assumption or hypothetical condition must be disclosed in conjunction with statements of each opinion or conclusion that is affected.

(ix)   **state the appraisal procedures followed, and the value opinion(s) and conclusion(s), and reference the workfile;**

Comment: An appraiser must maintain a specific, coherent workfile in support of a Restricted Use Appraisal Report. The contents of the workfile must be sufficient for the appraiser to produce a Summary Appraisal Report. The file should be available for inspection by the client (or the client's representatives, such as those engaged to complete an appraisal review), state enforcement agencies and such third parties as may be authorized by due process of law, and a duly authorized professional peer review committee. The review of a Restricted Use Appraisal Report in compliance with STANDARD 3 is not possible without the reviewer having benefit of the information retained in the workfile.

When the purpose of an assignment is to develop an opinion of market value, information analyzed in compliance with Standards Rule 1-5 is significant information that must be disclosed in a Restricted Use Appraisal Report. If such information was unobtainable, a statement on the efforts undertaken by the

STANDARD 2 (continued)

appraiser to obtain the information is required. If such information is irrelevant, a statement acknowledging the existence of the information and citing its lack of relevance is required.

(x) **state the use of the real estate, existing as of the date of value, and the use of the real estate reflected in the appraisal; and, when the purpose of the assignment is market value, state the appraiser's opinion of the highest and best use of the real estate;**

Comment: The report must contain a statement of the property use as is and as reflected in the appraisal, and the appraiser's opinion as to the highest and best use of the real estate, unless an opinion as to highest and best use is unnecessary, e.g. insurance valuation or "value in use" appraisals. If an opinion of highest and best use is required, the appraiser's reasoning in support of the opinion must be stated in the depth and detail required by its significance to the appraisal or documented in the workfile and referenced in the report.

(xi) **state and explain any permitted departures from specific requirements of STANDARD 1; state the exclusion of any of the usual valuation approaches; and state a prominent use restriction that limits use of the report to the client and warns that the appraiser's opinions and conclusions set forth in the report cannot be understood properly without additional information in the appraiser's workfile;**

Comment: When the DEPARTURE RULE is invoked, the assignment is deemed to be a Limited Appraisal. Use of the term Limited Appraisal makes it clear that the assignment involved something less than, or different from the work that could have and would have been completed if departure had not been invoked. The report of a Limited Appraisal must contain a prominent section that clearly identifies the extent of the appraisal process performed and the departures taken.

The Restricted Use Appraisal Report is for client use only. Before entering into an agreement, the appraiser should establish with the client the situations where this type of report is to be used, and should ensure that the client understands the restricted utility of the Restricted Use Appraisal Report.

(xii) **include a signed certification in accordance with Standards Rule 2-3.**

__Standards Rule 2-3__ **(This Standards Rule contains binding requirements from which departure is not permitted.)**

Each written real property appraisal report must contain a certification that is similar in content to the following form:

I certify that, to the best of my knowledge and belief:

-- **the statements of fact contained in this report are true and correct.**
-- **the reported analyses, opinions, and conclusions are limited only by the reported assumptions and limiting conditions, and are my personal, impartial and unbiased professional analyses, opinions, and conclusions.**
-- **I have no (or the specified) present or prospective interest in the property that is the subject of this report, and no (or the specified) personal interest with respect to the parties involved.**
-- **I have no bias with respect to the property that is the subject of this report or to the parties involved with this assignment.**
-- **my engagement in this assignment was not contingent upon developing or reporting predetermined results.**

STANDARD 2 (continued)

--   **my compensation for completing this assignment is not contingent upon the development or reporting of a predetermined value or direction in value that favors the cause of the client, the amount of the opinion, the attainment of a stipulated result, or the occurrence of a subsequent event directly related to the intended use of this appraisal.**

--   **my analyses, opinions, and conclusions were developed, and this report has been prepared, in conformity with the Uniform Standards of Professional Appraisal Practice.**

--   **I have (or have not) made a personal inspection of the property that is the subject of this report. (If more than one person signs the report, this certification must clearly specify which individuals did and which individuals did not make a personal inspection of the appraised property.)**

--   **no one provided significant real property appraisal assistance to the person signing this certification. (If there are exceptions, the name of each individual providing significant real property appraisal assistance must be stated.)**

Comment: A signed certification is an integral part of the appraisal report. An appraiser who signs any part of the appraisal report, including a letter of transmittal, must also sign this certification.

Any appraiser(s) who signs a certification accepts full responsibility for all elements of the certification, for the assignment results, and for the contents of the appraisal report.

When a signing appraiser(s) has relied on work from others who do not sign the certification, the signing appraiser is responsible for the decision to rely on those other's work. The signing appraiser(s) is required to have a reasonable basis for believing that those individuals performing the work are competent and that their work is credible.

The names of individuals providing significant real property appraisal assistance who do not sign a certification must be stated in the certification. It is not required that the description of their assistance be contained in the certification but disclosure of their assistance is required in accordance with S.R. 2-2(a), (b), or (c) (vii), as applicable.

Standards Rule 2-4 **(This Standards Rule contains specific requirements from which departure is permitted. See the DEPARTURE RULE.)**

An oral real property appraisal report must, at a minimum, address the substantive matters set forth in Standards Rule 2-2(b).

Comment: Testimony of an appraiser concerning his or her analyses, opinions, and conclusions is an oral report in which the appraiser must comply with the requirements of this Standards Rule.

See Record Keeping section of the ETHICS RULE for corresponding requirements.

STANDARD 3 REAL PROPERTY AND PERSONAL PROPERTY APPRAISAL REVIEW, DEVELOPMENT AND REPORTING

In performing an appraisal review assignment involving a real property or personal property appraisal, an appraiser acting as a reviewer must develop and report a credible opinion as to the quality of another appraiser's work and must clearly disclose the scope of work performed in the assignment.

> Comment: Appraisal review is the act or process of developing and communicating an opinion about the quality of all or part of a completed work or service performed by another appraiser in a real property or personal property appraisal assignment. The reviewer's opinion about quality must encompass the completeness, adequacy, relevance, appropriateness and reasonableness of the work under review, developed in the context of the requirements applicable to that work.
>
> The COMPETENCY RULE applies to the reviewer, who must correctly employ those recognized methods and techniques necessary to develop credible appraisal review opinions and also avoid material errors of commission or omission. A misleading or fraudulent appraisal review report violates the ETHICS RULE.
>
> Appraisal review requires the reviewer to prepare a separate report or a file memorandum setting forth the scope of work and the results of the appraisal review.
>
> The appraisal review requirements in this Standard do not apply to:
> - The activity of "review" or "audit" in the context of other professions, such as accounting;
> - An appraiser's study of work prepared by other types of experts, such as engineers or other consultants, or to work prepared by an appraiser in a consulting assignment under STANDARDS 4 and 5; and
> - review of an appraiser's work by non-appraisers, such as in "administrative reviews."

Appraisal reviewing is also distinctly different from the co-signing activity addressed in Standards Rules 2-5 and 8-5. To avoid confusion between these activities, a reviewer performing an appraisal review must not sign the work under review unless he or she intends to take the responsibility of a co-signer of that work.

Standards Rule 3-1 (This Standards Rule contains binding requirements from which departure is not permitted.)

In developing an appraisal review, the reviewer must:

(a)   identify the reviewer's client and intended users, the intended use of the reviewer's opinions and conclusions, and the purpose of the assignment;

> Comment: The intended use is in the context of the client's use of the reviewer's opinions and conclusions; for example, without limitation, quality control, audit, qualification, or confirmation. The purpose of the assignment relates to the reviewer's objective; for example, without limitation to evaluate compliance with relevant USPAP requirements, a client's requirements, or applicable regulations.
>
> A reviewer must ascertain whether the purpose of the assignment includes the development of his or her own opinion of value about the subject property of the work under review.
>
> If the purpose of the assignment includes the reviewer developing his or her own opinion of value about the subject property of the work under review, that opinion is an appraisal whether it:
>
> - concurs with the opinion of value in the work under review, as of the date of value in that work or a different date of value; or
> - differs from the opinion of value in the work under review, as of the date of value in that work or a different date of value.

STANDARD 3 (continued)

(b) **identify the:**

    (i)   **subject of the appraisal review assignment,**

    (ii)   **date of the review,**

    (iii)   **property and ownership interest appraised (if any) in the work under review,**

    (iv)   **date of the work under review and the effective date of the opinion in the work under review, and**

    (v)   **appraiser(s) who completed the work under review, unless the identify was withheld;**

<u>Comment</u>: The subject of an appraisal review assignment may be all or part of an appraisal report, the work file, or a combination of these.

(c) **identify the scope of work to be performed;**

<u>Comment</u>: A reviewer must take appropriate steps to identify the precise extent of the review process to be completed in an assignment. A reviewer must have sound reasons in support of the scope-of-work decision, and the resulting opinions and conclusions developed in the assignment must be credible and consistent with the intended use of the review.

In making the scope-of-work decision, the reviewer must identify any extraordinary assumptions necessary in the assignment. An extraordinary assumption may be used in an appraisal review assignment only if:

- it is required to properly develop credible opinions and conclusions;
- the reviewer has a reasonable basis for the extraordinary assumption;
- use of the extraordinary assumption results in a credible analysis; and
- the reviewer complies with the disclosure requirements set forth in SR 3-2(d) for extraordinary assumptions.

The appraisal review must be conducted in the context of market conditions as of the effective date of the opinion in work being reviewed. Information available to the reviewer that could not have been available to the appraiser as of or subsequent to the date of the work being reviewed must not be used by a reviewer in the development of an opinion as to the quality of work under review.

When the purpose of the assignment includes a requirement for the reviewer to develop his or her own opinion of value, the following apply:

- the reviewer's scope of work in developing his or her value opinion must not be less than the scope of work(Complete or Limited) applicable to the original appraisal assignment. However, the reviewer is not required to replicate the steps completed by the original appraiser. Those items in the work under review that the reviewer concludes are credible and in compliance with the applicable development standard (STANDARD 1 or 7) can be extended to the reviewer's value opinion development process on the basis of an extraordinary assumption by the reviewer. Those items not deemed to be credible or in compliance must be replaced with information or analysis by the reviewer, developed in conformance with STANDARD 1 or 7 as applicable, to produce a credible value opinion.
- the reviewer may use additional information available to him or her—either locally, regionally, or nationally—that was not available to the original appraiser in the development of his or her value opinion.

(d) **develop an opinion as to the completeness of the material under review within the scope of work applicable in the assignment;**

<u>Comment</u>: The reviewer is required to develop an opinion as to the completeness of the work under review within the context of the requirements applicable to that work.

STANDARD 3 (continued)

(e)   develop an opinion as to the apparent adequacy and relevance of the data and the propriety of any adjustments to the data;

(f)   develop an opinion as to the appropriateness of the appraisal methods and techniques used and develop the reasons for any disagreement;

(g)   develop an opinion as to whether the analyses, opinions, and conclusions in the work under review are appropriate and reasonable, and develop the reasons for any disagreement.

Standards Rule 3-2 (This Standards Rule contains binding requirements from which departure is not permitted.)

In reporting the results of an appraisal review, the reviewer must communicate each analysis, opinion, and conclusion in a manner that is not misleading:

> Comment: This rule addresses the content and level of information required in a report that communicates the results of an appraisal review. An appraisal review report is a supplementary critique intended for use in conjunction with the work under review.

> The reviewer must ensure that the client and any intended user of the assignment results will understand the review report and not be misled. A separate report or letter is one method. Another appropriate method is a form or checklist prepared and signed by the reviewer and attached to the work under review. It is possible that a stamped impression on an appraisal report under review, signed or initialed by the reviewer, may be used to reference a work file documenting the review.

In reporting the results of an appraisal review, the reviewer appraiser must

(a)   state the identity of the client, by name or type, and intended users; the intended use of the assignment results; and the purpose of the assignment;

(b)   state the information that must be identified in accordance with Standards Rule 3-1(b);

> Comment: If the identify of the appraiser(s) in the work under review was withheld, state that fact in the review report

(c))   state the nature, extent and detail of the review process undertaken (i.e., the scope of work identified in accordance with Standards Rule 3-1(c);

> Comment: When any portion of the work involves significant real or personal property appraisal or appraisal review assistance, the appraiser must state the extent of that assistance. The signing appraiser must also state the name(s) of those providing the significant real or personal property appraisal or appraisal review assistance in the certification in accordance with S.R. 3-2(f).

(d)   state the opinions, reasons, and conclusions required in Standards Rule 3-1 (d-g), given the scope of work identified in compliance with Standards Rule 3-1(c) ;

> Comment: When the purpose of an appraisal review assignment includes the reviewer expressing his or her own opinion of value, the reviewer must:

STANDARD 3 (continued)

1. state which information, analyses, opinions, and conclusions in the material under review the reviewer accepted as credible and used in developing the reviewer's opinion of value;

2. state any additional data relied upon, and the reasoning and basis for the reviewer's opinion of value; and

3. state any assumption, extraordinary assumption, limiting condition connected with the reviewer's opinion of value and, in accordance with Standards Rules 2-1 or 8-1 and 2-2 or 8-2(a), (b), or (c)(viii), as applicable, indicate the impact on value of any extraordinary assumption.

The reviewer may include his or her own value opinion within the appraisal review report itself without preparing a separate appraisal report. However, changes to the report content by the reviewer to support a separate value conclusion must match, at a minimum, the reporting requirements (Self-Contained, Summary or Restricted Use Appraisal Report) of the report under review.

(e)   include all known pertinent information; and

(f)   include a signed certification similar in content to the following:

I certify that, to the best of my knowledge and belief:

- --   **the facts and data reported by the reviewer and used in the review process are true and correct.**
- --   **the analyses, opinions, and conclusions in this review report are limited only by the assumptions and limiting conditions stated in this review report, and are my personal, impartial, and unbiased professional analyses, opinions, and conclusions.**
- --   **I have no (or the specified) present or prospective interest in the property that is the subject of this report, and no (or the specified) personal interest with respect to the parties involved.**
- --   **I have no bias with respect to the property that is the subject of this report or to the parties involved with this agreement.**
- --   **my engagement in this assignment was not contingent upon developing or reporting predetermined results.**
- --   **my compensation is not contingent on an action or event resulting from the analyses, opinions, or conclusions in, or the use of this review.**
- --   **my analyses, opinions, and conclusions were developed and this review report was prepared in conformity with the Uniform Standards of Professional Appraisal Practice.**
- --   **I did not (did) personally inspect the subject property of the report under review.**
- --   **no one provided significant real or personal property appraisal or appraisal review assistance to the person signing this certification. (If there are exceptions, the name of each individual(s) providing real or personal property appraisal or appraisal review assistance must be stated.)**

Comment: A signed certification is an integral part of the appraisal review report. An appraiser who signs any part of the appraisal review report, including a letter of transmittal, must also sign this certification.

Any appraiser(s) who signs a certification accepts full responsibility for all elements of the certification, for the assignment results, and for the contents of the appraisal report.

When a signing appraiser(s) has relied on work from others who do not sign the certification, the signing appraiser is responsible for the decision to rely on those other's work. The signing appraiser(s) is required to have a reasonable basis for believing that those individuals performing the work are competent and that their work is credible.

The names of individuals providing significant real or personal property appraisal or appraisal review assistance who do not sign a certification must be stated in the certification. It is not required that the description of their assistance be contained in the certification but disclosure of their assistance is required in accordance with S.R. 3-2(c).

Standards Rule 3-3 (This Standards Rule contains specific requirements from which departure is permitted. See DEPARTURE RULE.)

An oral appraisal review report must address the substantive matters set forth in Standards Rule 3-2.

Comment: Testimony of a reviewer concerning his or her appraisal review opinions and conclusions is an oral report in which the reviewer must comply with the requirements of this Standards Rule.

See the Record Keeping section of the ETHICS RULE for corresponding requirements.

Appendix B

Answers/Rationales for Review Questions

Preamble and Rules

1.   **B.** The standards contain binding requirements as well as specific requirements to which the Departure Rule *may* apply under certain limited conditions. Standards are for clients and intended users. USPAP does not set appraisal fees. *(Preamble, p. 123)*

2.   **C.** The minimum period for retention of records is five years following preparation or two years after final disposition, whichever period expires last. *(Ethics Rule, Record Keeping section, p. 126)*

3.   **A.** The Competency Rule requires the appraiser to have the knowledge and experience necessary to complete the assignment competently. *(Competency Rule, p. 127)*

4.   **B.** Feasibility analysis is defined as a study of the cost-benefit relationship of an economic endeavor. *(Definitions, p. 131)*

5.   **A.** The Departure Rule permits limited exceptions to sections of the standards if, among other requirements, this fact is clearly set forth in the report. *(Departure Rule, comment, p. 128)*

6.   **A.** The client is defined as the party or parties who engage an appraiser in a specific assignment. *(Definitions, p. 131)*

7.   **C.** As per the Ethics Rule, an appraiser has the obligation to promote and preserve public trust. *(Ethics Rule, p. 124)*

8.   **C.** A hypothetical condition is defined as that which is contrary to what exists but is supposed for the purpose of analysis *(Definition, p. 132)*

9.   **D.** Workfiles must, to a minimum, be retained for five years after preparation. *(Ethics Rule, Record Keeping section, p. 126)*

10.   **D.** The Departure Rule requires the appraiser to report any departure from specific requirements. *(Departure Rule, p. 128)*

11.   **A.** Three groups of persons are recognized under the Confidentiality Section. The groups include the client and persons specifically authorized by the client. *(Ethics Rule, Confidentiality section, p. 125)*

12.   **B.** The USPAP defines real property as the interests, benefits and rights inherent in the ownership of real estate. *(Definitions, p. 133)*

13.   **C.** The USPAP defines a report as "any communication, written or oral, of an appraisal, appraisal review, or consulting service that is transmitted to the client upon completion of an assignment." *(Definitions, p. 133)*

14.   **C.** The four sections of the Ethics Rule are: Conduct, Management, Confidentiality and Record Keeping. *(Ethics Rule, p. 124)*

15.   **B.** The Confidentiality Section of the Ethics Rule clearly identifies three persons (entities) to whom confidential factual data obtained from a client can be disclosed. Previous appraisers, and or owners, of the subject property are not listed nor is any reader of the appraisal report. *(Ethics Rule, Confidentiality section, p. 125)*

16.   **A.** Supplemental Standards *may* be issued by any public agency or client groups. The USPAP does not mandate that such groups issue standards. Appraisers and clients must ascertain whether supplemental standards apply to the appraisal assignment. *(Supplemental Standards, p. 129)*

Standard 1

1.   **D.** Standards Rule 1-4(e) does not require an appraiser to value the whole when the subject of the appraisal is a fractional interest; rather the appraiser must test and support the appropriateness of such analysis. All other choices in the question are binding requirements. *(Standards Rule 1-4(e), p. 137)*

2.   **A.** When applicable, the three approaches to value should be considered and used; however, nothing in the USPAP requires that all three of the traditional approaches to value be used if the subject matter is income-producing property or if a site is being appraised. The value being developed must simply be defined. *(Standards Rule 1-1(b), p. 134)*

3.   **A.** Standards Rule 1-5 requires an appraiser to examine any current agreement of sale, option or listing of the property being appraised if it is available in the normal course of business. *(Standards Rule 1-5(a), p. 138)*

4.   **A.** Certification that the appraisal report was prepared in conformity with the USPAP is a binding requirement under Standards Rule 2-3. The appraiser must identify easements and analyze the terms and conditions of the lease(s). *(Standards Rule 1-4(d), p. 137)*

5.   **A.** According to Standards Rule 1-1 (c), an appraiser must not render appraisal services in a careless or negligent manner. Necessary knowledge and experience is covered under the Competency Rule, confidentiality is addressed in the Ethics Rule, and the appraisal report is the subject of Standard 2. *(Standards Rule 1-1(c), p. 134)*

6.   **B.** The minimum periods for considering and analyzing prior sales is one year for one-to-four family residential property and three years for all other property types. *(Standards Rule 1-5(b)(i and ii), p. 138)*

7.   **C.** The continuing education hours are a part of the licensing/certification program of each jurisdiction, not USPAP. Social changes and changes in the development field both impact appraisal theory and practice. *(Standards Rule 1-1(a), p. 134)*

8.   **B.** The requirement that the appraisal contain sufficient information to enable the person(s) who receives the report to understand it properly is a binding requirement under Standards Rule 2-1. *(Standards Rule 1-1(c), p. 134)*

9.   **D.** The binding requirement of stating the name(s) of anyone who provided significant professional assistance to the person signing the report is not part of Standard 1. Sites should be valued by an appropriate method. *(Standards Rule 1-4(c)(iv), p. 137)*

10.   **C.** Certifying that the compensation received is not based on the reporting of a predetermined value is a binding requirement of Standards Rule 2-3. Examination of current sales should be done if available in the normal course of business. Land is appraised as though vacant and available for development to its highest and best use. *(Standards Rule 1-4(h)(i), p. 138)*

11.   **C.** Standard 1 contains five standards rules, three of which are binding requirements. Reports are the subject of Standard 2. *(Standard 1, pp. 134-139)*

12.   **B.** Standards Rule 1-3 is a specific requirement and it requires the appraiser to develop an opinion of the highest and best use of the real estate when the value opinion to be developed is market value. *(Standards Rule 1-3, pp. 136-137)*

13.   **C.** Standard 1 directs the appraiser to consider whether each use is applicable for the specific appraisal assignment. *(Standards Rule 1-4, p. 137)*

14.   **C.** Complete and limited appraisals are the two types of appraisals permitted under Standard 1. *(Definitions, p. 130)*

15.   **A.** A recertification of value is a limited appraisal performed for the purpose of confirming whether or not the completed improvements and/or market conditions are consistent with the assumptions and statements made in an earlier prospective appraisal. *(Definitions, p. 130)*

Standard 2

1.   **B.** A statement such as "The appraiser has no (or the specified) present or prospective interest in the property that is the subject of this report" or "I have (or have not) made a personal inspection of the property" would appear in the certification statement rather than in the assumptions and limiting conditions. *(Standards Rule 2-2(a)(viii), p. 141)*

2.   **B.** Nothing in Standard 2 either requires or suggests that the appraiser include in the certification statement the amount of the compensation he or she has received. The only mention of compensation is in regard to a statement that the compensation is not based on a contingency such as a direction in value that favors the client. Court testimony is an example of an assumption and limiting condition. *(Standards Rule 2-3, p. 147)*

3.   **C.** According to Standards Rule 2-3, an appraiser who signs any part of the appraisal report including a letter of transmittal must also sign the certification *(Standards Rule 2-3, p. 147)*

4.   **A.** Using recognized techniques in the development of an appraisal is addressed in Standard 1. Proper communication extends to intended users, not all readers. Both form and content are addressed in Standard 1. *(Standard 2, Comment, p. 139)*

5.   **C.** Standards Rule 2-3, which is a binding requirement, does not require the certification statement to be in a separate section of the appraisal report. However, a good practice would be to have the statement identified in a way that makes it clear to the client and the users of the report exactly what is being certified by the appraiser. The accuracy of sketches is addressed as an assumption and limiting condition. *(Standards Rule 2-3, Comment, p. 147)*

6.   **C.** Standards Rule 2-4, which addresses oral appraisal reports, is not a binding requirement. A certification statement is a binding requirement. *(Standard 2, Comment, p. 136; Standards Rule 2-3, p. 143; Standards Rule 2-4, p. 147)*

7.   **D.** Contingency compensation is not permitted in a real property appraisal assignment; thus, wording such as "my compensation is (or is not) contingent" would be inappropriate and misleading if included in the certification. Personal inspection and present interest are either "have" or "have not." *(Standards Rule 2-3, p. 146-147)*

8.   **C.** Standards Rules 2-2(a) requires the appraiser to define the value to be estimated. While market value may be the normal value being estimated, this is not always the case. Names of readers are not required, nor is the date of the last sale of the property. *(Standards Rule 2-2(a)(iv), p. 140)*

9. **C.** While the names of persons providing significant real property appraisal assistance to the person signing the certification must be stated, the amount of time spent by those persons does not have to be included in the certification. Persons providing clerical assistance do not have to be stated. *(Standards Rule 2-3, p. 146)*

10. **A.** The effective date establishes the context of the value opinion and could be a date prior to, equal to or after the date of the appraisal report. *(Standards Rule 2-2(a)(vi), p. 141)*

11. **D.** Assumptions and limiting conditions would include such a statement as "I assume that there are no hidden or unapparent conditions of the property that would render it more or less valuable." Personal inspection, compliance with the USPAP, and the fact that no one offered significant appraisal assistance would be part of the certification statement rather than part of the assumptions and limiting conditions. *(Standards Rule 2-2(a)(viii), p. 141)*

12. **C.** What makes an appraiser's efforts an appraisal are his or her "analysis, opinion and conclusion." *(Standard 2, p. 139)*

13. **D.** Standards Rule 2-4 states that as a minimum an oral real property appraisal must address the substantive matters set forth in Standards Rule 2-2(b). *(Standards Rule 2-4, Comment, p. 147)*

14. **A.** The three types of appraisal reports are self-contained, summary and restricted use. *(Standards Rule 2-2, p. 139)*

15. **C.** Complete/restricted use is an appraisal/appraisal report combination. *(Standards Rule 2-2, p. 139; Definitions, p. 130)*

Standard 3

1. **B.** A reviewer must take appropriate steps to identify the precise extent of the review process to be completed in an assignment. *(Standards Rule 3-1(c), p. 149)*

2. **A.** Standard 3 allows the reviewer to develop his or her own opinion of value. *(Standards Rule 3-1(c), Comment, p. 149)*

3. **B.** The review appraiser's compensation cannot be a contingency fee; therefore, the certification statement should say, "my compensation *is not* contingent on an action or event resulting from the analyses, opinions or conclusions in, or the use of, this review." Court testimony is a limiting condition. Standard 9 covers business appraisals. *(Standards Rule 3-2(f), p. 151)*

4. **C.** A misleading review clearly violates the Ethics Rule. Review appraisers do more than check for a level of completeness. The Competency Rule also applies to the reviewer. *(Standard 3, Comment, p. 148)*

5.   **D.** In reviewing an appraisal, the reviewer must develop an opinion as to the completeness of the material under review within the scope of work applicable in the assignment. *(Standards Rule 3-1(d), p. 149)*

6.   **B.** The striking difference between the appraisal of real or personal property and the review function is that the "review" standard is freestanding. Both the process of reviewing an appraisal and that of reporting the results of that review are covered in the same standard. *(Standard 3, Comment, p. 148)*

7.   **C.** The review appraiser should not sign the report under review unless he or she intends to take the responsibility of a cosigner. Both the Competency and Ethics Rules apply to review appraisers. *(Standard 3, Comment, p. 148)*

8.   **D.** Nothing in Standard 3 prohibits the reviewer from inspecting the subject property. Certification by the reviewer is a binding requirement. The names of those offering significant professional assistance must be stated. *(Standards Rule 3-2, p. 150)*

Answers/Rationales for Examinations

Examination I

1.   **C.** The conditions assumed under the definition of "market value" include the belief that all parties are acting in what they consider to be their best interests. *(Glossary, p. 14)*

2.   **C.** Assumptions and limiting conditions should not be confused with the certification statement. In this question, three of the choices are part of the appraiser's certification statement. *(Standards Rule 2-2(a)(viii), p. 141)*

3.   **A.** Oral testimony and reports fall under the Record Keeping Section of the Ethics Rule. The five– and two–year periods are minimums. Due process of law covers workfiles. *(Ethics Rule, Record Keeping section, Comment, p. 126)*

4.   **D.** Standard 9 addresses Business Appraisal, Development. *(Table of Contents, p. 121)*

5.   **B.** The requirements under the Competency Rule do not address the actions of a state appraisal board in terms of showing appraiser competency. *(Competency Rule, p. 127)*

6.   **C.** Comments are an integral part of the uniform standards and should be viewed as extensions of the rules, definitions and standards rules. *(Preamble, Comment, p. 123)*

7. **C.** An appraisal practice is defined by three terms in the USPAP: appraisal, appraisal review and appraisal consulting. *(Definitions, p. 130)*

8. **A.** USPAP requires that value be defined. The effective date of the appraisal must be included. The names of previous owners are not required to be included in the appraisal report. *(Standards Rule 2-2(a)(ii), p. 140)*

9. **C.** Standard 8 addresses the reporting of the results of a personal property appraisal by an appraiser. *(Table of Contents, p. 121)*

10. **C.** The minimum period for retention of records is five years following preparation or two years after final disposition, whichever period expires last. *(Ethics Rule, Record Keeping section, p. 126)*

11. **D.** The four sections of the Ethics Rule are: Conduct, Management, Confidentiality and Record Keeping. Departure is a separate rule. *(Ethics Rule, p. 124)*

12. **A.** Advisory opinions are informal responses to requests the ASB receives for information. An advisory opinion does not establish a new standard and is not enforceable; however, they have become exceedingly important. *(Preamble, p. 123)*

13. **A.** Contingency compensation in an appraisal consulting practice are unethical. Review appraisers are not permitted to accept contingency compensation. Contingency fees are addressed in the Management Section of the Ethics Rule. *(Ethics Rule, Management section, p. 125)*

14. **B.** Market value is the process of many real property appraisal assignments. *(Definitions, p. 132)*

15. **D.** Departure is not permitted with certification. Whether or not the property has been inspected must be stated, while clerical assistance need not be disclosed in the appraisal report. *(Standards Rule 2-3, p. 147)*

16. **C.** The Confidentiality Section includes parties authorized by due process of law. *(Ethics Rule, Confidentiality section, p. 125)*

17. **B.** Standards Rule 1-5 requires the appraiser to consider and analyze prior agreements of sale, *if* such information is available to the appraiser in the normal course of business. The time period is shorter for residential property, even though it is a minimum time frame. *(Standards Rule 1-5, p. 138)*

18. **A.** Standard 1 is directed toward the substantive aspect of developing a competent appraisal of real property. *(Standard 1, Comment, p. 134)*

19.   **B.** Personal property is defined as identifiable tangible objects that are considered by the general public as being "personal" and includes such items as furnishings or machinery and equipment. *(Definitions, p. 132)*

20.   **C.** Statements on standards are adopted by the ASB and serve to clarify, interpret, explain and/or elaborate standards and standards rules. *(Preamble, p. 123)*

21.   **D.** The Departure Rule permits limited exceptions to sections of the USPAP if, among other requirements, the appraiser clearly identifies and explains the departure(s). *(Departure Rule, p. 128)*

22.   **B.** Standard 4 addresses the performance of a real estate or real property consulting service. *(Table of Contents, p. 121)*

23.   **A.** The USPAP defines an "appraisal review" as the act or process of developing and communicating an opinion about the quality of another appraiser's work. *(Definitions, p. 130)*

24.   **A.** For one-to-four family residential property, an appraiser must examine prior sales for a minimum period of one year. *(Standards Rule 1-5(b), p. 138)*

25.   **C.** Investment analysis is defined as a study that reflects the relationship between acquisition price and anticipated future benefits of a real estate investment. *(Definitions, p. 132)*

Examination II

1.   **A.** Confidentiality is one of the four sections of the Ethics Rule. Departure Rule, Jurisdictional Exception Rule and Competency Rule are not part of the Ethics Rule. *(Ethics Rule, p. 124)*

2.   **A.** The USPAP was developed by the appraisal profession rather than a regulatory agency. The standards are for appraisers and the users of appraisal services. *(Preamble, p. 123)*

3.   **D.** Standards Rule 2-3 *requires* that the name of each individual providing significant real property appraisal assistance to the person signing the report must be stated. The appraiser may or may not have inspected the property. Appraiser compensation must not be contingent on predetermined opinions of value. *(Standards Rule 2-3, p. 146)*

4.   **D.** Market value assumes the price represents the normal consideration for the property sold, unaffected by special or creative financing granted by anyone associated with the sale. Reasonable time is assumed. Both parties are assumed to be well informed. *(Glossary, p. 14)*

5.   **B.** Standard 2 is the "reporting" standard for a real property appraisal. *(Standard 2, p. 139)*

6.   **A.** The USPAP defines real estate as an identified parcel or tract of land, including improvements, if any. *(Definitions, p. 133)*

7.   **D.** As per Standards Rule 2-3, an appraiser who signs any part of the appraisal report, including a letter of transmittal, must also sign the certification. *(Standards Rule 2-3, p. 147)*

8.   **D.** The Competency Rule requires the appraiser to have the knowledge and experience necessary to complete the assignment competently. *(Competency Rule, p. 127)*

9.   **D.** The revocation of an appraiser's certification by an appraisal board is not an example of an extraordinary assumption or limiting condition as intended in Standard 2. Atypical financing of the subject property should be included. *(Standards Rule 2-2(a)(viii), p. 141)*

10.   **C.** Appraisal consulting is defined as the act or process of developing an analysis, recommendation or opinion to solve a problem where an opinion of value is a component of the analysis leading to the assignment results. *(Definitions, p. 130)*

11.   **B.** Standard 5 addresses the reporting of the results of a real estate or real property consulting service by an appraiser. *(Table of Contents, p. 121)*

12.   **C.** Standards Rule 2-3 requires a certification statement *similar* in content to the one presented. The certification developed by a particular appraiser does not have to use the exact words and in fact most certification statements will be lengthier than the example used in Standards Rule 2-3. *(Standards Rule 2-3, p. 146)*

13.   **B.** The minimum period of time to be considered is one year for one-to-four family residential property and three years for all other property types. This is a binding requirement. *(Standards Rule 1-5(a), p. 138)*

14.   **C.** Records must be retained for five years following preparation or two years following final disposition, whichever period expires last. *(Ethics Rule, Record Keeping section, p. 126)*

15.   **B.** While some of the standards rules are binding requirements and thus departure is not permitted, certain standards rules are specific requirements to which, under certain conditions, departure is permitted. They are lengthier than the standards and many of them are followed by explanatory comments. *(Preamble, p. 123)*

16.   **D.** Three terms are used in the definitions of an appraisal practice. Those terms are "appraisal," "appraisal review" and "appraisal consulting." *(Definitions, p. 130)*

17.   **D.** Market analysis is defined as a study of market conditions for a specific type of property. *(Definitions, p. 132)*

18.   **C.** The appraiser should use his or her judgment and, therefore, should know if and when a particular approach to value is not appropriate for a specific appraisal assignment. S.R. 2-2(a)(xi) requires the appraiser to explain and support the reason for excluding any of the usual valuation approaches. *(Standards Rule 2-2(a)(xi), p. 142)*

19.   **C.** The four sections of the Ethics Rule are: Conduct, Management, Confidentiality and Record Keeping. *(Ethics Rule, p. 124)*

20.   **C.** If an appraiser discovers he has a lack of experience necessary to complete an appraisal assignment competently after having accepted the assignment, he may decide to withdraw from the appraisal assignment; however, the Competency Rule does not require *automatic* withdrawal by the appraiser. He or she must notify the client of the lack of experience. *(Competency Rule, Comment, p. 127)*

21.   **D.** The USPAP defines "appraisal review" as the act or process of developing and communicating an opinion about the quality of another appraiser's work. *(Definitions, p. 130)*

22.   **C.** Standard 7 addresses the development of a personal property appraisal. *(Table of Contents, p. 121)*

23.   **D.** Advisory opinions do not establish new standards and are unenforceable. Statements on standards have the same weight as standards rules. *(Preamble, p. 123)*

24.   **C.** For all properties other than one-to-four family residential property, an appraiser must examine prior sales for a minimum period of three years. *(Standards Rule 1-5(b)(ii), p. 138)*

25.   **D.** Standard 10 addresses the reporting of business appraisals. *(Table of Contents, p. 121)*

Appendix C

Answers/Rationales for Case Studies

Case 1

A.   **Has Bob made an appraisal?**

      Yes. From the Definitions Section of the USPAP, an appraisal is defined as "the act or process of developing an opinion of value. . . ." Bob estimated a minimum value of $2,250,000; however, he did not commit to a specific value estimate above that amount. Bob instructed his client, the developer, to tell the lender that the estimated value would be for more than the developer needed. Bob has acted as a disinterested third party in this situation and has represented a value estimate above a predetermined minimum.

B.   **Has Bob violated any of the sections of the USPAP? If yes, what has he violated?**

      Yes. Bob has violated several sections of the USPAP. He has violated the Conduct Section of the Ethics Rule. The Conduct Section states that:

> An appraiser must perform assignments ethically and competently in
> accordance with these standards, and must not engage in criminal conduct.
> An appraiser must perform assignments with impartiality, objectivity, and
> independence and without accommodation of personal interests.

      Bob has taken this assignment to accommodate his personal interest based on the fee of $20,000. In addition, Bob has violated the Management Section of the Ethics Rule that states, "Whenever an appraiser develops an opinion of value, it is unethical for the appraiser to accept compensation in developing that opinion that is contingent upon a direction in value that favors the cause of the client..." Bob has taken the fee based on finding a value that favors the cause of the client.

      Finally, assuming Bob takes this assignment and completes the appraisal report, he has violated Standards Rule 2-3, which addresses the minimum certification to be included in an appraisal report. He has violated the certification "My compensation for completing this assignment is not contingent upon the reporting of a predetermined value or direction in value that

Case 1 (continued)

> favors the cause of the client, the amount of the value opinion, the attainment of a stipulated result, or the occurrence of a subsequent event."

C.   **If you answered "yes" to Question B, what should Bob have done when the developer explained what he was trying to do?**

Bob should have explained to the developer that he (the developer) should go to the financial institution of his (the developer's) choice and arrange for financing subject to an appraisal. The financial institution then could employ Bob to complete the appraisal report with the institution as Bob's client. (The institution as client is required by the financial institution regulatory agencies.) If the developer wanted an idea or indication of a broad range of sales prices, he could initially employ Bob on an hourly basis for consulting time. Bob could report sales prices and a general range of sales prices for similar properties without stating an opinion of value.

Case 2

A.   **Has Jane violated any section or provision of the USPAP? Explain.**

Yes. Jane has violated several sections of the USPAP. She has violated the Conduct Section of the Ethics Rule. The Conduct Section states that:

> An appraiser must perform assignments ethically and competently in accordance with these standards, and not engage in criminal conduct . An appraiser must perform assignments with impartiality, objectivity, and independence and without accommodation of personal interests.

Jane has taken this assignment to accommodate her personal interest based on getting her property taxes lowered.

Jane also has violated Standards Rule 2-3, which addresses the minimum certification to be included in an appraisal report. She has violated the certification "My compensation for completing this assignment is not contingent upon the development or reporting of a predetermined value or direction in value that favors the cause of the client, the amount of the value opinion, the attainment of a stipulated result, or the occurrence of a subsequent event directly related to the intended use of this appraisal." In addition, Jane has violated Standards Rule 2-3, which states, "I have no (or the specified) present or prospective interest in the property that is the subject of this report, and no (or the specified) personal interest with respect to the parties involved." Jane was clearly biased in favor of herself and her neighbors and she had an interest in her own property.

Case 2 (continued)

B.   **Regardless of your answer in Question A, what should Jane have included in the certification statement accompanying each appraisal report?**

Jane should have disclosed in the certification statement that she lived in the neighborhood and that she would benefit from lower property taxes as a result of lower property values. In the appraisal report on her residence, Jane should have disclosed her present ownership interest.

Case 3

A.   **According to the USPAP, has Ed made an appraisal? Explain why or why not.**

There are arguments both in favor of and opposed to Ed's actions constituting an appraisal. Ed has represented to independent third parties that this is a value opinion, stated in terms of a standard unit of comparison—price per square foot. To develop an appraisal, Ed must perform an analysis of the data, develop an opinion and arrive at a conclusion. From the case, it appears that Ed reported sales information and did some analysis (from his comments, "probably about the same"). It is unclear as to whether Ed developed a value conclusion. (Some would argue that $2.00 to $2.10 per square foot constituted a value range.)

In the authors' opinion, Ed made an appraisal on two occasions. First, Ed gave an oral report when he ran into his old college buddy, Bob. Oral reports are governed by Standards Rule 2-4 and must conform, to the extent possible, to the requirements for a written report presented in Standards Rule 2-2. Second, Ed confirmed this oral report with subsequent written statements sent to Bob. Bob relied on the report as Ed had represented to a client that this was a value range for the subject.

B.   **If he has made an appraisal, which rules or standards rules has he violated?**

In terms of an oral report, Ed has violated Standards Rule 2-4, which states, "An oral real property appraisal report must, at a minimum, address the substantive matters set forth in Standards Rule 2-2(b)."

In terms of a written restricted use appraisal report, Ed has violated Standards Rule 2-2(c), parts (i) through (xii), and Standards Rule 2-3.

C.   **Would your answers to Questions A and B have been the same had Ed not collected the $200 fee?**

Yes. The amount of the fee is irrelevant to Ed's violation of the USPAP.

Case 4

A. Can Frank appraise the property without a set of plans and specifications?

No. According to Standards Rule 1-4 (h), Frank can "appraise proposed improvements only after examining and having for future examination: (i) plans, specifications, or other documentation sufficient to identify the scope and character of the proposed improvements; (ii) evidence indicating the probable time of completion of the proposed improvements; and (iii) reasonably clear and appropriate evidence supporting development costs, anticipated earnings, occupancy projections, and the anticipated competition at the time of completion."

B. Can Frank appraise the property as if it were fully occupied?

No. According to Standards Rule 1-4 (c)(iv), Frank must "base projections of future rent and expenses on reasonably clear and appropriate evidence." Unless Frank has market evidence to indicate instant 100 percent occupancy (which is highly unlikely), he cannot assume instant occupancy. Furthermore, Standards Rule 1-4 (h) (iii) requires the appraiser to appraise proposed improvements only after examining and having for future examination "reasonably clear and appropriate evidence supporting development costs, anticipated earnings, occupancy projections, and the anticipated competition at the time of completion."

Frank has been asked to make a prospective value estimate (at a date in the future), which is addressed in Statement on Appraisal Standards Number 4. Statement 4 reiterates, supports, and adds clarification to Standards Rule 1-4 (h).

C. Does the below-market interest rate impact the appraised value?

Assuming that Frank was engaged to estimate market value, below-market financing has no effect on market value. The definition of market value from the Glossary of the USPAP assumes that the "price represents the normal consideration for the property sold unaffected by special or creative financing or sales concessions granted by anyone associated with the sale."

Standards Rule 1-2(c) also applies to this situation. It requires the appraiser to define the value to be developed and if the value opinion to be developed is market value, the appraiser must clearly set forth any financing effects.

If Frank was engaged to estimate investment value, then he should clearly show the effects of special financing.

D. What standards rules cover plans and specs, full occupancy and below-market financing?

Standards Rule 1-4(h) covers appraising from plans and specifications as well as full occupancy. In addition, Statement on Appraisal Standards Number 4 addresses prospective value

Case 4 (continued)

estimates. Below-market financing is addressed in the Glossary of the USPAP and in Standards Rule 1-2 (d). Standards Rule 2-2(a)(b)(c)(xi) requires the appraiser to set forth this information in the appraisal report to adhere to or clearly identify and explain permitted departures from Standard 1.

E.   **Should Frank accept this appraisal assignment under the conditions and constraints stated?**

No. Frank should not accept this assignment if the client desires an opinion of market value. However, if the client desires an opinion of investment value, Frank may accept the assignment.

Case 5

A.   **Do the uniform standards apply to Phillip?**

Yes. In most instances, the USPAP applies to Phillip.

B.   **If your answer to Question A is "yes," explain how they apply since he does not make mention of them in his appraisal reports.**

If Phillip's appraisal reports are considered to be part of a federally related transaction, then he must conform to the USPAP. Title XI of FIRREA requires all real estate appraisal reports on federally related transactions to conform to the USPAP and to be written. Each state has passed, as part of its appraiser licensure/certification statute, a requirement for adherence to the USPAP in federally related transaction. More and more states are requiring adherence to USPAP for all real estate appraisals, not just those considered to be federally related transactions.

C.   **Can Phillip be forced to reference the USPAP in his appraisal reports? Explain.**

Yes. Phillip must include a minimum certification found in Standards Rule 2-3 of the USPAP on all real estate appraisal reports on federally related transactions since such reports must comply with the USPAP. In addition, the minimum requirements for the contents of the written appraisal reports found in Standards Rule 2-2 must be included.

Case 6

A.   **By not including a separate section on highest and best use in the appraisal report has Christine violated any part of the USPAP? Explain.**

Christine should have included a copy of the highest and best use section in her report. She did not violate Standard 1 for she considered highest and best use in her analyses. However, by failing to place a copy of the highest and best use section in the report, Christine violated Standards Rule 2-2(a)(b)(c)(x), which requires the appraiser to "describe the support and rationale for the appraiser's opinion of the highest and best use of the real estate. . . ." The comment section of 2-2(a)(x) also requires the appraiser's reasoning in support of the opinion to be included. Christine omitted both the reasoning and the conclusion from the report.

B.   **What should she do now that she has discovered her mistake?**

Once she discovered her mistake, Christine should send the client the highest and best use section and ask the client to attach the section to the original report.

Case 7

A.   **Does Jane have to inspect the property as part of the appraisal assignment?**

Jane is not required by the USPAP to physically inspect the subject. However, Standards Rule 2-3 requires her to disclose the fact that she did not personally inspect the subject.

B.   **If your answer to Question A is "no," then what steps should she take to fully comply with the USPAP?**

Jane must simply disclose the fact that she did not personally inspect the subject. The appropriate place for disclosure is in the certification statement.

C.   **What documentation should Jane include in her report to show the steps she has taken to complete the assignment as directed?**

Jane should document the directive of the lender to "go ahead and do the best job you can and not to worry about actually inspecting the property."

Case 8

A.   **Can Pete accept this type of compensation?**

Yes. Pete can accept this assignment and this type of compensation.

B.   **Has Pete violated any sections of the USPAP?**

Pete has not violated any sections of the USPAP; he merely is taking a percentage of a previously negotiated flat fee. The fee charged by the national appraisal firm is a flat fee for each appraisal and Pete is to receive 65 percent of that flat fee.

Case 9

A.   **Who is Ken's client?**

Don is Ken's client because he ordered the appraisal report and he is the party to whom Ken must look for payment.

B.   **Should Ken have given the opinion of value to Sarah over the telephone? Why or why not?**

No. Ken should not have given the opinion to anyone over the telephone. The Confidentiality Section of the Ethics Rule of the USPAP states that "an appraiser must not disclose confidential factual data obtained from a client or the results of an assignment prepared for a client to anyone other than: (1) the client and persons specifically authorized by the client. . . ." Don was Ken's client and Don did not specifically authorize Ken to provide Sarah with a value estimate. Statement on Appraisal Standards Number 5 reiterates this concept when it states:

> The results of an assignment prepared for a client are the appraiser's analyses, opinions, and conclusions pertinent to the assignment. These are clearly confidential matters under USPAP and may only be disclosed to the three groups cited in the *Comment* to the *Confidentiality* section.

C.   **What if Don had called? Should Ken have given him the opinion of value over the telephone? Why or why not?**

Ken should not have given a value opinion over the telephone. How could Ken be sure that it was Don on the telephone? In addition, giving Don a value opinion constituted an oral report that is governed by Standards Rule 2-4. Ken clearly violated Standards Rule 2-4 by not, at a minimum, addressing the substantive matters set forth in Standards Rule 2-2(b).

Case 9 (continued)

D.   **Which standards, if any, may have been violated by Ken?**

Ken may have violated Standards Rule 2-4 concerning an oral report, Standards Rule 2-2(a)(b)(c) concerning the required minimum contents of a written report, and Standards Rule 2-3 concerning the minimum certification in an appraisal report. Moreover, Ken clearly violated the Confidentiality Section of the Ethics Rule and the Statement on Appraisal Standards Number 5.

Case 10

A.   **Is Roger in violation of any rule or standard of the USPAP?**

Roger violated the Management Section of the Ethics Rule of the USPAP. The Management Section states that "Advertising for or soliciting appraisal assignments in a manner which is false, misleading, or exaggerated is unethical." Roger stated "all types of properties appraised" in his brochure, which was clearly exaggerated because he had not appraised the two types of properties shown in the brochure.

Roger also may violate the Competency Rule if he accepts appraisal assignments based on the brochure. If Roger has never appraised a particular type of property, he must disclose his lack of competency prior to accepting the assignment.

B.   **Assuming Roger had indeed appraised both of these properties, could he include a picture of them in his brochure without being in violation of the USPAP?**

As long as Roger does not represent that he has appraised "all types of properties," the inclusion of the pictures is not a violation of the USPAP per se. The pictures do not violate the Confidentiality Section, nor do they violate the Statement on Appraisal Standards Number 5.

Case 11

A.   **Has Mike violated any part of the USPAP?**

Yes.

B.   **If your answer to Question A is "yes," what has he violated?**

He has violated the Record Keeping Section of the Ethics Rule.

Case 11 (continued)

C.   **How long should Mike keep the information in his files?**

      According to the Record Keeping Section of the Ethics Rule, Mike "must prepare a workfile for each assignment and retain the workfile for a period of at least five (5) years after preparation or at least two (2) years after final disposition of any judicial proceeding in which testimony was given, whichever period expires last." Based on the USPAP, Mike should keep copies of his workfile until February 7, 2004.

      The state where Mike lives may have a record-keeping requirement that is longer than the one in the USPAP. If this is true, Mike must abide by his state's statute. For example, his state could require an appraiser to retain all copies of reports and testimony for six (6) years following final disposition.

Case 12

A.   **Does that "other stuff" apply to Larry? Explain.**

      Yes. The "other stuff" does indeed apply if this is a federally related transaction. Section 1110 of Title XI of FIRREA requires financial institution regulatory agencies (including the OCC) to prescribe appropriate standards for appraisal reports. These guidelines require, at a minimum, adherence to the USPAP and that all real estate appraisal reports be written. However, financial institution regulatory agencies have the right, power, and authority to impose additional requirements on appraisal reports pursuant to Section 1110 of Title XI. Each financial institution's regulatory agency has developed final appraisal rules that impose additional requirements.

B.   **Is Larry in violation of the USPAP if he does not incorporate regulatory agency guidelines and rules into his appraisal assignments and reports?**

      Yes. Larry is in violation of the Supplemental Standards Rule.

C.   **How might Larry stay abreast of regulatory agency guidelines considering the fact that such rules and regulations seem to be constantly changing?**

      Larry could subscribe to the Appraisal Foundation's subscription service. For a small annual fee, the Foundation will send him pronouncements of the Appraisal Subcommittee of the Federal Financial Institutions Examination Council. He should also check with his clients to see if they are aware of any supplemental standards.

Case 13

A.   **Should Ray accept this appraisal assignment?**

Ray may accept this assignment.

B.   **By accepting the second appraisal assignment has Ray violated any rules in the uniform standards? Explain.**

Ray has not violated any provisions in the USPAP by accepting this assignment. The two assignments are for two different parcels and Ray does not have an interest in either parcel.

C.   **Is Ray obligated under the USPAP to inform the fast-food chain of the results of this previous appraisal?**

No. If Ray does inform them of the results of a previous appraisal on a nearby parcel, Ray would violate the Confidentiality Section of the Ethics Rule.

Ray also could use data from prior research so long as that research did not contain confidential data. Ray could operate under the assumption that data from a previous report was not confidential unless that previous client specifically told Ray that it was confidential or Ray had reason to believe it was confidential. This opinion is based on the Statement on Appraisal Standards Number 5.

Case 14

A.   **Is Beth fulfilling the requirements of the Competency Rule when she accepts this assignment? If not, what should she do?**

No. She is not fulfilling the requirements of the Competency Rule. To be competent, Beth must have both the knowledge and experience to complete the assignment competently. If she is not competent, prior to accepting the assignment or entering into any agreement for services, she must disclose her lack of competency, take the necessary steps to become competent, and describe the actions taken in the appraisal report.

B.   **Is Beth competent to accept this assignment? What if the apartment complex was only 50 units, rather than 250?**

Beth is not competent to take this assignment based on being a certified residential appraiser. A certified residential appraiser is competent to appraise one-to-four family residential

Case 14 (continued)

property. Whether the subject is 50 or 250 units is irrelevant if Beth is only a certified residential appraiser.

C.   **By accepting this assignment, has she violated any rules of the USPAP?**

        Yes. She has violated the Competency Rule.

Case 15

A.   **Should Billy accept this appraisal assignment?**

        Yes. Billy may accept the assignment; however, he must comply with the Competency Rule in the USPAP.

B.   **If your answer to Question A is "yes," what makes Billy competent to accept the assignment?**

        Billy is not competent to complete this assignment. He should inform the client, prior to taking the assignment, that he lacks the knowledge and/or experience to complete the assignment competently. If the client tells Billy to proceed, Billy must take the necessary steps to become competent. These necessary steps include personal study by the appraiser, affiliation with another appraiser who is competent for this type of assignment, or retention of an expert. Finally, Billy must describe in the appraisal report his lack of competency and the actions taken to become competent.

C.   **How does the "knowledge and experience" criteria mentioned in the Competency Rule relate to the fact that the "world's expert" on appraising boat marinas had to appraise the first one at some point in time?**

        The Competency Rule is intended to inform clients about an appraiser's training or lack of training for a given assignment. The burden is on the appraiser to inform the client, to allow the client to make a choice regarding selection of an appraiser, and to put any reader of the report on notice that the appraiser was not competent at the inception of the assignment to complete it competently. However, because of certain steps taken by the appraiser and disclosed in the report, the appraiser has become competent for property types similar to the subject in that geographic area.

Case 16

A.   **Because Marshall has retired, was he still obligated to save his workfiles? Explain.**

    If Marshall's appraisal reports were prepared according to the USPAP, he represented to clients that he would retain copies of reports for a minimum of five (5) years following preparation or two (2) years following final disposition in any legal proceeding in which testimony was given, whichever period expires last. This is based on the minimum requirements established in the Record Keeping Section of the Ethics Rule.

B.   **Since Marshall is now retired, is there any jurisdiction over him in case someone complains to the state appraisal board that Marshall did not keep his records as required by the USPAP?**

    Most states require adherence to the USPAP as a statutory requirement beginning with that state's appraiser licensure/certification statute. Since Marshall is no longer certified by the state, there is some question as to whether or not the state appraisal board can regulate his past activities.

C.   **What would you suggest to Marshall?**

    Marshall should retain a copy of his reports and all file memoranda for a minimum period of five (5) years following preparation or two (2) years following final disposition in any legal proceeding in which testimony was given, whichever period expires last. Moreover, if his state appraiser licensure/certification statute requires a longer period, Marshall should adhere to this longer period; this would show compliance with the Jurisdictional Exception Rule in the USPAP.

Case 17

A.   **Has Susan done anything wrong?**

    Yes. She has violated the USPAP, and in the case of a federally related transaction, she has violated her state appraiser licensure/certification statute.

B.   **Has she violated any sections of the Ethics Rule?**

    Yes. She has violated the Conduct Section of the Ethics Rule. The Conduct Section states, "An appraiser must perform assignments with impartiality, objectivity, and independence and without accommodation of personal interests." Susan is acting as an independent, unbiased third party rendering appraisal services. If her fee were dependent on closing of the loan, she has a vested interest to "come in with a value estimate that the client wants in order to do the deal."

Case 17 (continued)

The Management Section of the Ethics Rule also is applicable in this situation. It states:

Whenever an appraiser develops an opinion of value, it is unethical for the appraiser to accept compensation in developing that opinion that is contingent upon ... a direction in value that favors the cause of the client.

Susan has taken the fee based on finding a value that favors the cause of the client.

Finally, assuming Susan takes this assignment and completes the appraisal report, she has violated Standards Rule 2-3, which is the minimum certification to be included in an appraisal report. She has violated the certification that states, "my compensation for completing this assignment is not contingent upon the development or reporting of a predetermined value or direction in value that favors the cause of the client, the amount of the value opinion, the attainment of a stipulated result, or the occurrence of a subsequent event directly related to the intended use of this appraisal."

C.   **What should Susan tell the financial institution in terms of her need to be in compliance with the USPAP?**

She should inform the institution that she must be independent, objective and impartial. As such, she should be paid for professional services rendered, regardless of whether the loan closes.

Case 18

A.   **Should Martha accept this appraisal assignment?**

No.

B.   **If your answer to Question A is "no," why should she not accept it?**

Martha should not accept the assignment for two reasons. First, if the contract rent is less than the market rent, Martha could have a financial interest in the property because her leasehold estate could have value. The leasehold estate is the tenant's interest in a leased property and has value when the market rent exceeds the contract rent and is recognized by the marketplace. Second, Martha might be biased, either positively or negatively, toward the building.

Case 18 (continued)

C.   **Would there be conditions under which Martha could accept this assignment? Explain.**

Yes, if Martha disclosed her possible financial interest and her possible biases pursuant to Standards Rule 2-3. This is an appraisal for investment value and Martha should note this in the report and comment on any possible effects from bias.

Case 19

A.   **How many "small errors" does it take before an appraiser is in violation of the USPAP? Explain.**

One "small error" that is misleading is a violation of the USPAP. Standards Rule 1-1 (c) requires the appraiser to "not render appraisal services in a careless or negligent manner, such as by making a series of errors that although individually might not significantly affect the results of an appraisal, in the aggregate affect the credibility of those results." If John's careless mistakes are misleading, then he has violated the USPAP.

B.   **Does the USPAP require John to correct these errors and resubmit the appraisal reports?**

No. The USPAP does not specifically address the correction of mistakes in previously issued reports. However, professionalism and common sense dictate that John should correct and resubmit these reports.

C.   **Would the institution have a legitimate complaint against John? Explain.**

Yes. The institution would have a legitimate complaint against John for violation of Standards Rule 1-1 (c).

Case 20

A.   **Can Richard accept the assignment and still be in compliance with the USPAP?**

Yes. Under the Jurisdictional Exception Rule, Richard would be allowed to accept the assignment and complete it pursuant to the judge's instructions. Because the subdivision or land development method is not acceptable under case law, Richard must abide by state law. The Jurisdictional Exception Rule specifically states, "If any part of these standards is contrary to the law or public policy of any jurisdiction, only that part shall be void and of no force or effect in that

Case 20 (continued)

jurisdiction." Ordinarily, the subdivision or land development method is a preferable method for the valuation of sites in a new development. However, because of case law, this method is unacceptable in Richard's state.

B.   **Can Richard make an appraisal given the instructions of the judge, and if so, is Richard in violation of the USPAP if he follows the orders of the court?**

Yes. He can make an appraisal and is not in violation of the USPAP. He must simply cite the Jurisdictional Exception Rule in his appraisal report.

C.   **What does the USPAP say in regard to recognized appraisal methods not being used because of court decisions?**

Court decisions are not specifically addressed in the USPAP. However, in this case Richard should clearly include the judge's instructions in the appraisal report.

Case 21

A.   **Has Don violated any of the provisions of the Ethics Rule? If the answer is "yes," what has he violated?**

Yes. Don has violated the Conduct and Management Sections of the Ethics Rule. The Conduct Section states:

An appraiser must perform assignments ethically and competently in accordance with these standards and must not engage in criminal conduct. An appraiser must perform assignments with impartiality, objectivity, and in-dependence and without accommodation of personal interests.

Don is "working with the developer" or at least instructing those appraisers who work for him to "work" with the developer for his (Don's) personal gain.

In addition, Don has violated the Management Section, which states, "Whenever an appraiser develops an opinion of value, it is unethical for the appraiser to accept compensation in developing that opinion that is contingent upon ... a direction in value that favors the cause of the client." By "working with the developer," Don has violated the Management Section of the Ethics Rule. In addition, Don violated Standards Rule 2-3 because he represented in the certification that this was his unbiased estimate that did not favor the cause of the client.

Case 21 (continued)

B.   **If your answer to Question A is "yes," would your answer have been the same if Don did not sign the report? Explain.**

Yes. The Conduct and Management Sections of the Ethics Rule make no reference to a signature on an appraisal report. Rather, they refer to actions of the appraiser. As a result, Don would be in violation of the Ethics Rule of the USPAP regardless of whether he signed the report.

C.   **If your answer to Question A is "yes," would your answer have been the same if Don did not receive any of the fee? Explain.**

Yes. Don would be in violation of the Conduct Section of the Ethics Rule. However, Don would not be in violation of the Management Section of the Ethics Rule because he accepted no compensation. Violation of the Management Section is based on the acceptance of compensation which states:

an appraiser must not communicate assignment results in a misleading or fraudulent manner. An appraiser must not use or communicate a misleading ora fraudulent report or knowingly permit an employee or other person to communicate a misleading or fraudulent report.

Case 22

A.   **Is Joe in violation of the USPAP? Explain.**

Joe is in violation of Standard 3, Standards Rules 3-1 and 3-2. In the comment section to S. R. 3-1(c), the review appraiser "must take appropriate steps to identify the precise extent of the review process. To be completed in an assignment" Standards Rule 3-1 specifies the minimum steps in the review process, while Standards Rule 3-2 specifies the minimum reporting requirements in a review report.

B.   **If Joe is in violation of the USPAP, as a review appraiser what should he have done if he disagreed with the estimate of value?**

The comment section to Standards Rule 3-2(d) states that "when the purpose of an appraisal review assignment includes the reviewer expressing his or own opinion of value, the reviewer must: (1) state which information, etc the reviewer accepted as credible; (2) state any additional data relied upon, and the reasoning and basis for the reviewer's opinion of value; and (3) state any assumption, extraordinary assumption, and limiting condition connected with the reviewer's opinion of value."

Case 23

A.   **Is Marti in violation of any rules of the USPAP?**

Yes. Marti has violated Standards Rule 1-2 (e)(iv) and Standards Rule 2-2 (a)(b)(c)(iii). Standards Rule 1-2 (e)(iv) requires the appraiser to "identify any known easements . . . ." The comment section to Standards Rule 2-2(a)(b)(c)(iv) includes the following wording: "the statement of the real property rights being appraised must be substantiated, as needed, by copies or summarizes of title descriptions or other documents that set forth any known encumbrances." Because an easement is an encumbrance, Marti should have included a copy in the appraisal report.

B.   **Does the USPAP require the appraiser to render any legal opinion? Explain.**

No. The appraiser is not permitted by state statute to render a legal opinion, unless the appraiser is also a duly licensed member of the bar.

C.   **Could/should Marti have included a statement in her limiting conditions section that would cover her omission of the easement in the appraisal report?**

Many appraisers place limiting conditions in their reports. However, if the USPAP imposes a requirement, appraiser's limiting conditions will not supersede the USPAP's requirements.

Case 24

A.   **According to the USPAP, must Bryant show his work to a professional peer review committee?**

According to the USPAP, Bryant would not be forced to show his work to a professional peer review committee. However, he would be allowed to show it under the Confidentiality Section of the Ethics Rule. An appraiser may disclose a confidential report or data to three parties, one of which is a duly authorized professional peer review committee except when such disclosure to a committee would violate applicable law or regulation.

Case 24 (continued)

B.   **If he refuses to give the professional peer review committee the appraisals, has Bryant violated any rule of the USPAP?**

No. However, he probably will not receive his designation. The USPAP allows Bryant to give the professional peer review committee a copy of his reports—it does not force him to do so.

C.   **According to the USPAP, what should Bryant do?**

He should give copies to the professional peer review committee, but disclose to the committee his confidentiality letter.

D.   **If copies of Bryant's appraisals are given to members of the professional peer review committee, what obligations, if any, do committee members have to Bryant?**

As stated under the Confidentiality Section of the Ethics Rule, "It is unethical for a member of a duly authorized professional peer review committee to disclose confidential information or factual data presented to the committee."

Case 25

A.   **Is the $20,000 a contingency fee? Explain.**

Yes. The $20,000 is a contingency fee. Gerald must complete the work within three days and estimate a value of at least $1,200,000. The fee is contingent on both events. Both the $1,200,000 and the time factor are contingencies.

B.   **Given the directive by the client that the company needs the work "within three days for at least $1,200,000," can Gerald accept the assignment?**

No. If Gerald accepts this assignment, he will be in violation of the Management Section of the Ethics Rule of the USPAP. He will be accepting compensation contingent on reporting a value estimate that favors the cause of the client and the attainment of a stipulated result. In addition, he will be violating the minimum disclosure requirements imposed by Standards Rule 2-3.

Case 25 (continued)

C.   **What should Gerald do to comply with the USPAP?**

He should not agree to a floor amount of $1,200,000 as a contingency for the $20,000. A higher than normal fee for speed of service (three days) is fine, but it should not be coupled with a minimum pre-specified value estimate.

Case 26

A.   **Has the appraiser violated the USPAP?**

Yes. The appraiser has violated portions of the USPAP.

B.   **If your answer to Question A is "yes," what rules have been violated?**

The appraiser has violated the Confidentiality Section of the Ethics Rule. Clearly Ken, the borrower, is the appraiser's client. Ken ordered the appraisal report and paid the appraiser. The ordering of the appraisal by Ken points to his being the client of the appraiser.

C.   **What should the appraiser have done? Explain.**

The appraiser should have received written permission from Ken, the client, to allow the appraiser to give a copy of the appraisal to the financial institution. The written permission should have been signed by Ken. In addition, since this is a federally-related transaction, the appraiser should have informed Ken that the appraisal must be ordered by the institution and not by the borrower.

Case 27

A.   **Has Morris violated the USPAP? Explain.**

The answer to this question is not an easy "yes" or "no" answer. The appraiser has violated the USPAP if he did not disclose that he was not competent in the geographic area of the appraisal assignment. This lack of competency has nothing to do with his mental abilities or his knowledge of property types in other geographic areas where he has worked. However, the answer to the question could be "no" if the appraiser spends sufficient time to understand the local market

Case 27 (continued)

nuances. The client needs to acknowledge the fact that the appraiser has disclosed that the appraiser has not appraised this type property in this specific market.

B.   **If Morris accepts the assignment, what could he do to protect himself from recourse by the client?**

Once Morris receives written acknowledgment from the client regarding the appraiser's lack of geographic experience, the written acknowledgment should be made part of his workfile and retained as per the Record Keeping Section of the Ethics Rule.

Case 28

A.   **If the appraiser does as instructed has she violated the USPAP? Explain.**

In both instances ("readdress" or "reissue") there would be a violation of the Confidentiality Section of the Ethics Provision unless the financial institution releases the appraisal report. The original financial institution was the client assuming it ordered the appraisal report and paid the appraiser. If, however, the person seeking the financing ordered and paid for the appraisal, the appraiser has also violated the USPAP by giving the appraisal to the financial institution and not the person who paid for the appraisal. (The reader should also be aware of Advisory Opinion G-3 which addresses the appropriateness of an update of an appraisal).

B.   **Must the appraiser readdress the appraisal to the second lender?**

No. The appraiser does not have to follow the instructions of the second lender.

Case 29

A.   **Have you violated any of the rules of the USPAP? If the answer is "yes," what have you violated and why?**

No. An evaluation is a limited appraisal and limited appraisals are addressed by the USPAP. What you must do is clearly disclose that you are conducting a limited appraisal assignment. Accordingly, you must follow the binding requirements of the USPAP with particular attention paid to S.R. 2-2 and S.R. 2-3. S.R. 2-2 requires you to prominently state which appraisal report option (Self-Contained, Summary, or Restricted Use) you are using. In addition, you must follow the Departure Rule.

Case 29 (continued)

B.   **Do "evaluations" fall under state appraisal statutes?**

Yes and no. In some states, the definition of a real estate appraisal includes "evaluations" while in other states it does not. (Please check your specific state appraisal statute).

Case 30

A.   **Can the bank give a copy of the appraisal without Steve's permission? Explain.**

This question is not addressed by the USPAP. USPAP does not address the lending functions of financial institutions; rather, it addresses appraiser requirements. Lender requirements are the subject of the various regulatory rules and if you are engaged by any financial institution, you should have a copy of the applicable regulatory rules. The giving of an appraisal by a financial institution to a borrower has been addressed in FDIC Improvement Act of 1991 which says "each creditor shall promptly furnish an applicant upon written request by the applicant made within a reasonable period of time of the application, a copy of the appraisal report used in connection with the applicant's application for a loan that is or would have been secured by a lien on residential property. The creditor may require the applicant to reimburse the creditor for the cost of the appraisal."

B.   **If the bank gives the borrower a copy of the appraisal report, is Steve now obligated to answer questions he receives directly from the borrower?**

No. If, and when, the borrower acquires a copy of the appraisal report, regardless of how it is required, the lender still remains the client of the appraiser.

Appendix D

Appraisal-Related Web Sites

This is a listing of the web addresses for a number of major appraisal associations, sources and related groups. These sites can serve as good reference and information sources and offer links to still other organizations. Practicing appraisers may investigate the societies as a way of establishing professional credentials and keeping up-to-date in the field. Many of these organizations publish professional journals or newsletters, hold meetings and seminars, and offer member designations. Understand that this compilation is not all-inclusive as there are many other national and local Internet sites that focus on appraisal. Also realize that this information is subject to change at any time.

Appraisal-Related Web Sites

Appraisal Foundation (www.appraisalfoundation.org)
Not-for-profit corporation that establishes, promotes and improves appraisal standards and qualification criteria through the use of two independent boards: the Appraiser Qualifications Board (AQB) and the Appraisal Standards Board (ASB). In addition, the Appraisal Foundation improves the report option (Self-Contained, Summary, or Restricted Use) you are using. In addition, you must follow the Departure Rule.

Appraisal Institute (www.appraisalinstitute.org)
Sets minimum standards for appraisers and fosters professionalism through designation programs that recognize knowledge, training and experience in residential and commercial appraisal.

Appraisal Subcommittee (www.asc.gov)
Government entity charged with overseeing the activities of the Appraisal Foundation and state appraiser regulatory programs. Maintains a national registry of licensed and certified appraisers authorized to perform federally related transactions.

Association of Appraiser Regulatory Officials (www.aaro.net)
Organization of state appraiser regulatory agencies and appraisal-related groups that seeks to improve the administration and enforcement of appraisal laws in member jurisdictions.

Foundation of Real Estate Appraisers (www.frea.com)
Professional organization offering a benefits program for practicing appraisers, including E&O insurance and continuing education. Includes home inspectors and environmental assessors in its membership.

National Association of Independent Fee Appraisers (www.naifa.com)
Not-for-profit organization promoting networking, cooperation and fellowship among its members.

American Society of Farm Managers and Rural Appraisers (www.asfmra.org)
Group representing professionals in the valuation, financial analysis and management of agricultural and rural resources.

American Society of Appraisers (www.appraisers.org)
Full-service association representing many disciplines of appraisal specialists, including real estate valuation. Provides education, testing and accrediting programs.

Appendix E

State Real Estate Appraiser Boards

From time to time you may find it necessary to contact an appraiser board other than the one in your particular jurisdiction. The names, addresses, and telephone numbers of all appraiser boards are provided in this appendix. The personnel at the board should be able to answer your questions dealing with appraisal regulatory matters over which that board has jurisdiction. Keep in mind that this information is subject to change.

State Real Estate Appraiser Boards

Alabama

James W. Holland, Jr.
Executive Director
Alabama Real Estate Appraiser Board
P. O. Box 304355
Montgomery, AL 36130-4355
(334) 242-8747 (O)
(334) 242-8749 (F)
www.agencies.state.al.us/reab/

Alaska

Jenny McElwain
Administrator
Alaska Board of Certified Real Estate Appraisers
P.O. Box 110806
Juneau, AK 99811-0806
(907) 465-2542 (O)
(907) 465-2974 (F)
www.dced.state.ak.us/

Arizona

Edward Logan
Executive Director
Arizona Board of Appraisal
1400 West Washington, Suite 360
Phoenix, AZ 85007
(602) 542-1565 (O)
(602) 542-1598 (F)
www.appraisal.state.az.us

Arkansas

Jim Martin
Executive Director
Arkansas Appraiser Licensing and
Certification Board
2725 Cantrell Road, Suite 202
Little Rock, AR 72202
(501) 296-1843 (O)
(501) 296-1844 (F)

California

Anthony Majewski
Director
Office of Real Estate Appraisers
1755 Creekside Oaks Drive, Suite 190
Sacramento, CA 95833-3637
(916) 263-0881 (O)
(916) 263-0886 (F)
www.test:cahwnet.gov/orea

Colorado

Stewart A. Leach
Program Administrator
Colorado Board of
Real Estate Appraisers
1900 Grant Street, Suite 600
Denver, CO 80203
(303) 894-2166 (O)
(303) 894-2683(F)
www.dora.state.co.us/real-estate

Connecticut

Lauren Rubino
Real Estate Examiner
Real Estate Appraisal Commission
165 Capitol Avenue, Room 110
Hartford, CT 06106
(860) 713-6150 (O)
(860) 713-7630 (F)

Delaware

Louise Holt
Administrative Assistant
Delaware Council on Real Estate Appraisers
Professional Regulation Division
Cannon Bldg, Suite 203
Dover, DE 19903
(302) 739-4522 (O)
(302) 739-2711 (F)

District of Columbia

Dorothy Thomas
Administrator
DCRA/OPLA
941 N. Capitol Street, NE
Washington, DC 20002
(202) 442-4472 (O)
(202) 442-4528 (F)

Florida

Charlotte Hattaway
Regulation Program Administrator
Florida Real Estate Appraisal Board
400 West Robinson Street
North Tower, Suite N308
Orlando, FL 32801-1772
(407) 245-0800 (O)
(407) 317-7035 (F)
www.state.fl.us/dbpr

Georgia

Charles Clark
Real Estate Commissioner
Georgia Real Estate Commission
International Tower, Suite 1000
229 Peachtree Street, NE
Atlanta, GA 30303-1605
(404) 656-3916 (O)
(404) 656-0529 (F)
www.greab.state.ga.us

Hawaii

Candice Ito
Executive Officer
Hawaii Real Estate Appraiser Advisory Com
P. O. Box 3469
Honolulu, HI 96801
(808) 586-2704 (O)
(808) 586-2689 (F)

Idaho

Thomas Limbaugh
Bureau Chief
Idaho State Certified Real Estate Appraisers Bd
Bureau of Occupational Licensing
1109 Main St., Suite 220
Boise, ID 83702-5642
(208) 334-3233 (O)
(208) 334-3945 (F)
www.2.state.id.us/ibol/rea

Illinois

Michael Brown
Appraisal Administrator
Illinois Office of Banks and Real Estate
310 S. Michigan Ave., Suite 2130
Chicago, IL 60604
(312) 793-3000 (O)
(312) 793-8720 (F)
www.obre.state.il.us/

Indiana

Julie Wiesinger
Board Coordinator
Indiana Professional Licensing Agency
302 W. Washington, Room EO 34
Indianapolis, IN 46204
(317) 232-7209 (O)
(317) 232-2312 (F)
www.state.in.us/pla/appraiser/index.html

Iowa

Susan Griffel
Executive Officer
Professional Licensing and
Regulation Division
Department of Commerce
1918 Southeast Hulsizer Avenue
Ankeny, IA 50021-3941
(515) 281-7417 (O)
(515) 281-7411 (F)
www.state.ia.us/iapp

Kansas

Sally Pritchett
Executive Director
Kansas Real Estate Appraisal Board
1100 S.W. Wanamaker Rd., Suite 104
Topeka, KS 66604
(785) 271-3373 (O)
(785) 271-3370 (F)
www.ink.org/public/kreab

Kentucky

Sam E. Blackburn
Executive Director
Kentucky Real Estate Appraisers Board
1025 Capitol Center Drive, Suite 100
Frankfort, KY 40601-8205
(502) 573-0091 (O)
(502) 573-0093 (F)
www.state.ky.us/govtinfo

Louisiana

Anne Brassett
Administrative Assistant
Louisiana Real Estate Commission
P. O. Box 14785
Baton Rouge, LA 70898-4785
(504) 925-4783 (O)
(504) 925-4431 (F)

Maine

Carol Leighton
Administrator
Maine Board of Real Estate Appraisers
State House Station #35
Augusta, ME 04333
(207) 624-8520 (O)
(207) 624-8637 (F)
www.state.me.us/pfr/led/appraisers/index.htm

Maryland

Charles P. Kazlo
Executive Director
Maryland Real Estate Appraisers Commission
500 N. Calvert Street, Room 302
Baltimore, MD 21202
(410) 333-6328 (O)
(410) 333-6314 (F)
www.dllr.state.md.us/occprof/reappr.html

Massachusetts

Judith H. Meltzer
Program Coordinator
Board of Real Estate Appraisers
239 Causeway Street, Suite 500
Boston, MA 02114
(617) 727-3055 (O)
(617) 727-2197 (F)
www.state.ma.us/reg/board/ra

Michigan

Judith A. Dennis
Licensing Administrator
Michigan Board of Real Estate Appraisers
P.O. Box 30018
Lansing, MI 48909-7519
(517) 241-9201 (O)
(517) 241-9280 (F)
www.cis.state.mi.us

Minnesota

Scott Borchert
Enforcement Supervisor
Minnesota Commerce Department
85 N. 7th Place #500
St. Paul, MN 55101
(651) 296-9431 (O)
(651) 284-4106 (F)
www.commerce.state.mn.us

Mississippi

Robert Praytor
Administrator
Mississippi Real Estate Appraiser and
Certification Board
2506 Lakeland Drive, Suite 300
Jackson, MS 39208
(601) 932-9191 (O)
(601) 932-3880 (F)
www.mab.state.ms.us

Missouri

Roger Fitzwater
Executive Director
Missouri Real Estate
Appraisers Commission
P.O. Box 1335
Jefferson City, MO 65102-1335
(573) 751-0038 (O)
(573) 526-2831 (F)
www.ecodev.state.ma.us/pr/rea/

Montana

Lorri Sandrock
Board Administrator
Montana Board of Real Estate Appraisers
P. O. Box 200513
Helena, MT 59620-0513
(406) 841-2386 (O)
(406) 841-2305 (F)
www.commerce.mt.gov/license/pcl/nonmed/rea/index.htm

Nebraska

Marilyn Hasselbalch
Executive Director
Nebraska Real Estate Appraiser Board
P.O. Box 94963
Lincoln, NE 68509-4963
(402) 471-9015 (O)
(402) 471-9017 (F)
dbdec.nrc.state.ne.us/appraise

Nevada

Brenda Kindred-Kipling
Appraisal Officer
Department of Business and Industry
Nevada Real Estate Division
788 Fairview Drive, Suite 200
Carson City, NV 89701
(775) 687-4280 (O)
(775) 687-4868 (F)
www.state.nv.us/b&i/red

New Hampshire

Sally Sullivan
Executive Secretary
Real Estate Appraisal Board
State House Annex, Room 426
25 Capitol Street
Concord, NH 03301-6312
(603) 271-6186 (O)
(603) 271-6513 (F)

New Jersey

James Hsu
Executive Director
State Board of Real Estate Appraisers
Department of Law and Public Safety
P.O. Box 45032
Newark, NJ 07101
(973) 564-6480 (O)
(973) 564-6458 (F)
www.state.nj.us/lps/ca/nonmed/htm

New Mexico

Ricardo Campos
Board Administrator
New Mexico Real Estate Appraisers Board
P. O. Box 25101
Santa Fe, NM 87504
(505) 476-7100 (O)
(505) 476-7094 (F)
www.rld.state.nm.us/rld/asd.htm

New York

Keith Stack
Deputy Secretary to the Board
New York Board of Real Estate Appraisers
84 Holland Avenue
Albany, NY 12208-3490
(518) 474-4429 (O)
(518) 473-6648 (F)
www.dos.state.ny.us/lcns/licensing

North Carolina

A. Melton Black, Jr.
Executive Director
North Carolina Appraisal Board
P.O. Box 20500
Raleigh, NC 27619-0500
(919) 420-7920 (O)
(919) 420-7925 (F)
www.NCAB.state.nc.us

North Dakota

Jodie R. Campbell
Executive Director
North Dakota Appraisal Board
P.O. Box 1336
Bismarck, ND 58502-1336
(701) 222-1051 (O)
(701) 222-8083 (F)

Ohio

Sylvia A. Keberle
Administrative Assistant
Ohio Real Estate Appraisal Board
615 Superior Avenue NW, Rm 525
Cleveland, OH 44113
(216) 787-3100 (O)
(216) 787-4449 (F)
www.com.state.oh.us/real

Oklahoma

Michelle Shadid-Dobbs
Director
Oklahoma Real Estate Appraiser Board
P. O. Box 53408
Oklahoma City, OK 73152-3408
(405) 521-6636 (O)
(405) 522-0125 (F)

Oregon

Robert A. Keith
Appraiser Compliance Program Coordinator
Appraiser Certification & Licensure Board
530 Center St., NE, Suite 305
Salem, OR 97301
(503) 373-1505 (O)
(503) 378-6576 (F)
www.cbs.state.or.us

Pennsylvania

Cheryl B. Lyne
Board Administrator
State Board of Certified Real Estate Appraisers
P.O. Box 2649
Harrisburg, PA 17105-2649
(717) 783-4866 (O)
(717) 787-7769 (F)

Rhode Island

Valerie Voccio
Administrator
Rhode Island Real Estate Appraisers Board
233 Richmond Street, Room 230
Providence, RI 02903-4230
(401) 277-2262 (O)
(401) 277-6654 (F)

South Carolina

Robert L. Selman
Administrator
Real Estate Appraisers Board
P.O. Box 11847
Columbia, SC 29211-1847
(803) 896-4400 (O)
(803) 896-4404 (F)
www.llr.sc.edu/reab

South Dakota

Sherry Bren
Administrator
Appraiser Certification Program
Department of Commerce/Regulation
118 West Capitol
Pierre, SD 57501-2000
(605) 773-4608 (O)
(605) 773-5369 (F)
www.state.sd.us/dcr/appraisers

Tennessee

Sandy Moore
Administrative Director
Tennessee Real Estate Appraiser Commission
500 James Roberson Parkway, 6th Floor
Nashville, TN 37243-1166
(615) 741-1831 (O)
(615) 253-1692 (F)
www.state.tn.us/commerce/treac

Texas

Renil C. Liner
Commissioner
Appraiser Licensing and Certification Board
P.O. Box 12188
Austin, TX 78711-2188
(512) 465-3950 (O)
(512) 465-3953 (F)
www.talcb.capnet.state.tx.us

Utah

Ted Boyer
Director
Utah Department of Commerce
Division of Real Estate
160 East 300 South
Salt Lake City, UT 84114-6711
(801) 530-6762 (O)
(801) 530-6749 (F)
www.commerce.state.ut.us/web

Vermont

Theodore McKnight
Board Administrator
Vermont Real Estate Appraisers Board
109 State Street
Montpelier, VT 05609-1106
(802) 828-3228 (O)
(802) 828-2368 (F)
www.vtprofessionals.org/appraisers

Virginia

Karen W. O'Neal
Assistant Director
Real Estate Appraiser Board
Department of Professional
and Occupational Regulation
3600 West Broad Street, 5th Floor
Richmond, VA 23230-4817
(804) 367-2039 (O)
(804) 367-2475 (F)
www.state.va.us/dpor

Washington

Cleotis Borner, Jr.
Program Manager
Real Estate Appraiser Section
Business and Professions Division
P.O. Box 9015
Olympia, WA 98507-9015
(360) 753-1062 (O)
(360) 586-0998 (F)
www.wa.gov/dol/bpd/appfront.htm

West Virginia

Sharon Knotts
Executive Director
Appraiser Licensing and Certification Board
2110 Kanawha Blvd, Suite 101
Charleston, WV 25311
(304) 558-3919 (O)
(304) 558-3983 (F)
www.state.wv.us/appraise

Wisconsin

Katharine Hildebrand
Bureau Director
Wisconsin Real Estate Appraisers Board
P.O. Box 8935
Madison, WI 53708-8935
(608) 266-3423 (O)
(608) 267-3816 (F)
www.badger.state.wi.us.agencies/ddrl

Wyoming

Constance K. Anderson
Administrator
Certification Real Estate Appraiser Board
2020 Carey Avenue, Suite 100
Cheyenne, WY 82002-0180
(307) 777-7141 (O)
(307) 777-3796 (F)
www.realestate.state.wy.us